Stories of Real People
Succeeding Without Sight

Kristin Smedley

Thriving Productions
Ivyland, Pennsylvania

Thriving Blind
Stories of Real People
Succeeding Without Sight
By Kristin Smedley

Copyright 2019 ©by Kristin Smedley

Thriving Blind is available at special discounts for bulk purchases by schools, nonprofits, or other organizations. For more information please contact: Thriving Blind@gmail.com

Cover Design by Eric Labacz
www.labaczdesign.com

Published by Thriving Publications
Ivyland, PA

To the three people
Who are responsible for gray hairs on my head
And laugh lines on my face:
Michael Jr, Mitchell, and Karissa,
You show the world what thriving looks like every day
And you are the reasons I am thriving in my life.
God sent me the best of the best
When he sent the three of you to me.

To the two people
Who are responsible for
My resilience despite adversity:
Mom and Dad,
You've shown the world
How unconditional love sets us up to thrive.
Your constant support, cheering, and cleaning up my
kitchen
Have enabled me to thrive as a mom.
God sent me to the best of the best,
When he sent me to both of you.

I am blessed.

Contents

Foreword

By Erik Weihenmayer

My first reaction to Kristin Smedley's refreshing new book, *Thriving Blind*, was: "Wow! It's about time a parent lays out the fundamentals to a successful life for their blind children." Kristin would know. She's the mother of two blind boys, both born with a rare eye disease, Leber Congenital Amaurosis (LCA)—as Kristin said, "a double dose of darkness," and as a family member mused bitterly, "like winning the lottery twice."

However, Kristin's parental lens began to shift and her mind began opening to all the possibilities awaiting. She eloquently writes, "I was empowered to set extraordinary expectations." Clearly and frankly, she points out the key factor in the equation: her role as a parent. She beautifully presents how her beliefs and fears, her perspective and mindset, could become either her boys' biggest barrier or the boys' most powerful catalyst.

Kristin states that when someone wants something badly enough, they seek out the best resources and role models. That desire led her on a quest to meet blind people around the country who were living their dreams. About five years ago, I invited Kristin and her family to my house in Colorado. Young boys at the time, Michael and Mitchell tumbled around on our wrestling mat and climbed on my home climbing wall. We ate pizza, and the boys pet my guide dog, who was off duty, of course, as well as our three chickens. Kristin and family went away with a little more belief that an exciting and fulfilling life as a blind person was possible. Since then, Kristin has made it a point to meet successful blind women and men around the country. Some of them such as Tom Wlodkowski and Lonnie Bedwell are dear friends of mine. She illuminates their stories and dissects their positive traits in the chapters of *Thriving Blind*.

The results of Kristin's exploration are reflected in this book, but also in the lives of her boys who have played on championship baseball teams, taken honors classes, played and sung in bands, dated girls and gone to proms, and attended college. As Kristin writes, "Their lives are about their dreams."

The story of my family and me is strikingly similar. I describe my parents as the broom and the dustpan. My dad would sweep me out into the world only to be shattered. Then my mom would gather up the broken pieces and rebuild them, only to have my dad sweep me out again. It was a repeating anti-intuitive process of failure and fortification.

When initially diagnosed with a rare disease that the doctors said would take my sight completely as an early teen, my desperate mother brought me to an empty church, wrapped her arms around me, and prayed for a miracle that would restore my sight. As a little boy, I prayed alongside her—to see like my brothers, to catch a football, and to charge down the basketball court on a fast break. I prayed for sight so that my parents wouldn't bring me to dark places and sound so desperate and scared.

But just like Kristin, ultimately, my mom's attitude changed, and she became my biggest advocate for living a full life. She was a mother lioness fighting for my every opportunity. When I was about to start school, it was still rare for visually impaired children to be mainstreamed at a public school. Meeting with a group of close-minded administrators, my mom dug in and stated forcefully, "I have a distant cousin who was born prematurely. The incubator made her blind. You know what they taught her at the school for the blind? They taught her to tune pianos. Now there's nothing wrong with tuning pianos. It's perfectly respectable. The funny part is that my cousin was tone deaf." My mother burst into strained laughter. "You know what she does now?" My mom paused and then delivered each word separately and deliberately: "She does nothing. She can't make a bed or cook a meal. She can't even peel an orange by herself. And what's going to happen to the poor thing when her mama and daddy die? Where's she gonna go? What's she gonna do? Who's gonna peel her oranges then? My baby can move around the house and neighborhood on his own. He can take out the garbage and vacuum the floor. He can look at comic books. Puts his head right against the page, but he can see them. He can swim in the pool, dribble a basketball. He plays football with his brothers. They let him be quarterback and yell out, 'Erik, over here. This way,' and he throws it right to them. He's not going to tune pianos, and he's not going to sit around the house waiting for the dinner bell. He's going to go to a normal school, with normal children, and even if I have to go to school with him, he's going to learn."

I'll never know how my mom had the courage to so forcefully oppose the establishment. She knew very little about blindness. However, she believed in me. I was just a skinny little boy with thick glasses. I was an unwritten book. But somehow she saw strength, opportunity, and promise, while others saw only problems, obstacles, and limits. I thank her for that powerful belief every day.

My dad pushed me in other ways and taught me a lot about what I now call "a No Barriers Mindset." In middle school, with only very limited vision, I loved to perform stunts on my mountain bike. I'd sit at the top of my steep driveway wearing an Evel Knievel t-shirt and black leather gloves. After a few deep breaths, I'd launch myself down the drive, around the corner, and over a wooden ramp positioned at the bottom. I'd soar off the ramp and land on another ramp, eight feet past the first. Then I'd circle the cul-de-sac with one hand on the handle bar and the other raised victoriously in the air, waving to the imaginary crowd. But one day while pedaling back up the driveway for another jump, my bike and the ground seemed to swerve side to side, and I just managed to put my foot down before I toppled over. My vision was swimming and growing fuzzy. I told myself that I was only imagining my diminished sight, that it was only the temporary blinding flash of the sun in my eyes, anything but the truth. I tried to make the jump a few more times, but the ramp and the pavement beneath seemed to blend together. I'd either pop off the side of the ramp or miss altogether.

At the top of the driveway, my father was spray painting an old chest. Although I didn't notice him, he couldn't help but notice me. He grimaced each time I missed, wanting so badly to run down and command me to stop before I got hurt, but he held his ground. He knew he couldn't come running each time I confronted a challenge. Finally, he saw me give up in disgust and angrily push my bike into the garage. Saying nothing to my dad as I stormed inside, I slammed the door. My father looked at the dull wooden ramp and at the can of spray paint in his hand. Then he walked into the garage and studied the rack of different colored spray paints until his eyes stopped on bright orange.

The next day over breakfast, my father encouraged me to try the ramp again. I hesitantly pedaled down the driveway as he watched anxiously from the top. When I rounded the corner, I immediately noticed something vastly different. I could clearly see the outline of the ramp; it shone bright orange in the sun. I could smell the aerosol odor of spray paint as I hit the first ramp dead on, flew across the gap, and touched down on the landing ramp. Soon my confidence was back. I even convinced my two brothers to lie down on their stomachs between the ramps so that I could jump over them. They reluctantly agreed, and I'm happy to report that both of them survived.

With the right support, encouragement, and belief, your child will survive, too. In fact, as Kristin so poignantly describes, "They'll do better than survive. They will thrive."

Erik Weihenmayer is the author of three books, Touch the Top of the World, The Adversity Advantage, *and* No Barriers, *and is a filmmaker and prominent international speaker. Totally blind, he has climbed Mt. Everest and the Seven Summits, and kayaked the mighty rapids of the Grand Canyon. He is an ice climber, para-glider, skier, mountain biker, and has more than 50 skydives to his credit. He has been honored as National Geographic's Adventurer of the Year and was recently named one of the 25 greatest adventurers of the last 25 years. His greatest achievement is the founding of No Barriers 13 years ago, which now serves almost 10,000 challenged people annually. His message to young and old, challenged or not challenged, is to live a No Barriers Life. Erik resides with his wife Ellen and two children in Golden, Colorado.*
See www.touchthetop.com for more information.

A Double Dose of Darkness

An Introduction

I stood at the back of the large room setup in a typical conference style: a basic black stage with about a hundred plain folding chairs facing it. The room was split in half by an aisle down the middle of the perfectly lined up chairs. Typically at a conference I excitedly enter the space and bounce around the room to chat with folks and find a great seat. But not this time. Here I hesitated for a long while before making my way, ever so slowly, begrudgingly, down that aisle to look for a place to sit.

Although I didn't want to get too close to the front of the room or even anyone in the room, I needed to find a good seat where I could hear everything the presenters had to say. After all, I had a lot to learn. I didn't *want* to learn from them; I *needed* to learn from them. I walked closer to the front, my feet moving slower, slower. Walking away from the back of the room toward the stage, I was walking away from my dreams and into my nightmare.

Holding back tears as I looked around, I saw a group of empty seats on the right. Next to the seats were two parents apparently trying to please their daughter. I guessed she was about fourteen or fifteen years old. She sat with her feet up on her chair and her legs crossed in a format that the forever elementary school teacher in me calls "crisscross applesauce." She was rocking quickly, forward and back, forward and back. As she rocked, her mother handed her a drink.

"What is that? Is that orange juice? I didn't want orange juice!" she yelled.

Her mom, looking exhausted, apologized and said she would go find something better for her. Next, her father came to her with food.

"These aren't chocolate chip cookies! I said I want cookies! Chocolate chip!" she demanded. He quickly went back to the snack table to get the right cookies.

My heart pounded. My stomach was in a knot. I couldn't believe what I was seeing. I'm sure I didn't hide my look of horror. More upsetting was the fact that the others nearby witnessing this family didn't seem upset at all. Most had a look of understanding, an "I get it" look. Some even seemed to have a look of *acceptance* about what was happening.

Next, I glanced to the left of the aisle where there was another family sitting near a group of open seats. A mom and her perhaps thirteen-year-old son were in a heated argument. The boy was slumped in the chair, arms crossed, legs stretched out in front of him with his ankles crossed. His back was turned to his mom. She was whispering in what seemed an attempt to not cause a scene, but her voice was escalating. I leaned in to hear her.

"Absolutely not! It is completely inappropriate," the mother said.

"God, Mom—you don't let me do anything!" her son huffed.

"You are being completely obnoxious!" she scolded.

"Skateboarding is not obnoxious!" he fired back.

"Skateboarding in a hotel is obnoxious, unsafe, and RUDE," she replied.

This family was arguing over what was and was not appropriate in terms of skateboarding in a hotel! I was intrigued. I wanted—needed—to know more about them.

That conference was a meeting for families with children who are blind due to Leber Congenital Amaurosis

(LCA), a very rare eye disease causing blindness. The children in the families I encountered on either side of the aisle were blind. The girl who was upset with her family's "snack service" was blind. The young slumped-in-the-chair skateboarder was blind. And I was there because I had recently found out that my newborn son was blind, too. My baby, Michael, was diagnosed with LCA at five months old. This conference was my first experience meeting children like him, and moms like me.

Do you remember that scene in the movie "My Cousin Vinny" where Joe Pesci's character finally presents a great argument in court and wins over the courtroom—and the friend of his nephew stands up and shouts: "Him! I want him!"? Well, after witnessing the skateboarding argument I turned to my little family and yelled: "Here! I want to sit here!"

I wanted to sit with the family that looked and acted

> *I was consumed by the fact that my baby could not see. He couldn't see my smile. He couldn't see his toys. He was blind. That's all I thought about. My son was blind. Sigh. Cry. Repeat.*

"normal." Not that any of us are "normal" per se, but they didn't "act blind." They were having a typical family argument. The boy seemed like a typical teen. I wasn't interested in how he was able to skateboard without sight. I wasn't concerned about what else he enjoyed. I wanted to know more about the fact that their issue had nothing to do with blindness. Blindness wasn't mentioned at all. I thought, "How could that be?" At that point in my life, every second of every hour of every day I was consumed by the fact that my baby could not see. He couldn't see my smile. He couldn't see his toys. He was blind. That's all I thought about. My son was blind. Sigh. Cry. Repeat.

The encounters I had in that center aisle led to my first "aha moment" in my journey of raising blind children. While I didn't know a thing about raising a blind child, I decided that day that I wanted the kind of life in which I would debate skateboarding etiquette with my son, not whether I served him the correct juice or not! I made the choice at that moment to get myself as close as possible to people that I wanted to be like and I wanted my son to be like—moms, dads, and kids that were not just surviving blindness, but *thriving*. I wanted to know what they knew, do what they did.

Blindsided

I knew there was something not quite right about his eyes. Then, in the summer of the year 2000, in a little exam room at Children's Hospital of Philadelphia, I was told my baby was "very blind." I knew he was having some vision issues. But *blind*? I remember the doctor's stunned face when I asked: "Blind? How blind?" Then my second question: "What will he do?"

The answers were like bricks piling on my heart. No baseball. No driving. No normal life.

The news slammed me to the floor, literally. Since the moment I found out I was pregnant with Michael I pictured him as the starting pitcher, the football quarterback, and the class president. I envisioned a life of me cheering on the sidelines as he achieved his dreams, not him on the sidelines where life would pass him by. In that tiny room I was told the life I had planned for him was gone. While the doctor mentioned the white cane and Braille, I heard dependence and loneliness.

In that exam room in Philly, my family and I were given no hope, no resources, not even a pamphlet about how to raise a blind child. However, we were given the name of a doctor that we were told was the number one person in the United States for the rare eye disease my baby was suspected of having: LCA. As luck would have it, Dr. Irene Maumenee was on the East Coast at Johns Hopkins in Baltimore. Typically, it can take up to a year to get in to see a specialist of Dr. Maumenee's caliber. But nothing about my journey has been typical. Our local specialist made one phone call to Dr. Maumenee, and she made herself available to see us on short notice. The appointment with Dr. Maumenee turned out to be a pivotal moment in my family's journey with LCA and with my journey as a mom. Not only was Dr. Maumenee knowledgeable about our rare eye disease, she informed us about a small parent group she had been working with that was coordinating resources for LCA families. Dr. Maumenee encouraged me to contact the group and get involved in their online email support group for LCA parents. (In the year 2000 there was no Facebook or any social media platform to easily connect with others with a rare disease.) The listserv, the email support group, would become a wonderful resource to connect with other families.

I emailed the listserv group: "Hi. My name is Kristin. My baby was just diagnosed with LCA. I don't know any blind people and have no idea where to begin. Any advice would be wonderful." The group was very welcoming. Many members posted replies to console me and acknowledged the devastation they knew I was feeling. For two weeks, every time Michael slept I jumped on the email list to read posts. I stayed up all night to read them. Two weeks of posts that discussed "no light perception," schools for the blind, white canes, loneliness, developmental delays, education laws…oh dear God. Just two weeks prior I was searching online mommy groups for fun activity ideas; now I was weeding through the devastating messages about a life I couldn't wrap my head or heart around.

The email list is where I found information regarding the conference I mentioned in the opening of this book. The LCA family conference was full of families on a similar journey. The conference also had a few eye specialists available to talk about this rare disease. However, with so little known about the disease at that time, the majority of information was about coping with blindness and resources for raising blind children, nothing about hope for treatments or a cure or anything at all to make my baby not blind or even not *so* blind.

At the time when I entered the back of that conference room I was crying about this diagnosis every day. Every. Single. Day. I cried when I knew Michael wasn't seeing me smile at him. I cried over the thought of him trying to play with friends. I cried as I thought about typical preschool activities that my son would not be able to do. I couldn't face my friends who had "normal" kids. I couldn't face my future that seemed so dark. Although stepping into that conference room was excruciating, it was the step I needed to take to face my fears of raising a blind child. I was forced to immerse myself in the very topic I wanted no part of, but needed to know everything about. Fortunately, I met two people there who changed the trajectory of my journey in raising blind children: Kay Leahy and her blind son Patrick. You'll read about them and their impact on me later in this book.

Kay and Pat were the first of many people I have been blessed to have come into my journey and change my perception of possibility for my boys.

Boys. Plural. I actually have two sons that have LCA. Mitchell was born three years after my first son and was diagnosed with LCA, just like Michael. I used to call it a double dose of darkness. A family member says: "We hit the lottery twice" in a cynical tone. I believe we did win the lottery. Three times. I have a sighted daughter in addition to my blind sons. My three children have taught me more about perception, resilience, and inclusion than all of the books I have ever read. They have taught me more than any YouTube video or TED Talk I have ever watched. Keep reading and you'll see why.

Reach

When my first son was diagnosed with blindness, the root of my devastation was fear because I had never known a single blind individual. I had no idea what was possible for a blind person. The first blind person I met was my own son. The second was Patrick. The third was a super cool guy, Erik Weihenmayer.

Erik Weihenmayer's first big claim to fame (he's got a few!) is that he was the first blind person to summit Mt. Everest. You read that right: Erik is blind. He has no sight whatsoever. None. Nada. He can't see his hand in front of his face, yet he climbed the highest mountain. So what have you accomplished today?

The book *Touch the Top of the World* tells Erik's story of losing his sight in his teen years, getting angry, and eventually, my favorite part: accepting his blindness and rising strong, so strong. The pages of the first half of my copy of the book were saturated with my tears. It's **that** difficult of a journey. In fact, when I sent a copy of the book to my mom, she called me when she got about a third of the way through and was upset with me for sending her such a heart-wrenching story! I'll tell you what I told her: You have to keep going—the second half of the book, the part where Erik moves into acceptance and thriving, is so worth the agony you go through in the first half.

The second half of the book is full of details about mountain climbing. Frankly, I don't want my children to climb the highest peaks, thank you very much. However, as I read about Erik figuring out how to communicate with his team, and how to work around ice and snowstorms, my eyes opened wider and wider to the possibility of my sons being able to work around the obstacles that would surely come their way.

Presently, Erik has climbed the highest mountain on all

seven continents. He speaks around the globe about living life with "No Barriers," reaching for your dreams, and using adversity to your advantage. People call Erik "inspirational." But for me he's a life changer. Erik is successful. He is a husband and a dad. He is fun-loving, kind, and adventurous. But the best thing about Erik is that he is completely comfortable in his own skin. For me, he's all the things I hope my sons will become. All the things I thought were lost when I heard: "Your son is blind."

My family and I had an opportunity to visit with Erik and his family at their home in Colorado a few years ago. My children still talk about the wrestling mats, climbing walls, kayaks, and chickens (yes, chickens!). Interestingly, Erik is not just an inspiration to me, my boys, and people who are living with blindness. Erik is a wonderful example to my sighted daughter that her brothers will live normal lives (although Karissa will likely debate that her brothers are too annoying to be normal; sibling rivalry is alive and well at my house, too).

Ralph Waldo Emerson once said, "Our chief want is someone who will inspire us to be what we know we could be." I didn't realize how much I wanted that on the day of the first blindness diagnosis, how much I needed inspiration, and, well, **proof** regarding what a blind person could do, could be. As it turns out, a person without sight can do pretty much anything they want. Okay not *everything*. None of us can do everything. But you get what I mean, and you'll see proof of it in the coming chapters. Seventeen years ago, I didn't know about all of this possibility and options and "normalness" surrounding blindness. I had no idea that my sons would absolutely be able to achieve the greatness they are destined for.

Meeting Kay and Patrick opened my eyes to the possibilities for blind children. Meeting Erik blew the roof off of possibility. The most extraordinary thing is that Michael was only six years old when he met Erik. Children start out so innocently believing the world is at their fingertips. Michael was no exception. He had big dreams. Huge. That encounter with Erik kept Michael's mind open to dream and reach for all he wanted in life, as opposed to surrendering to the closed minds of people that wanted him to live within their limits and boundaries.

How I See It

So often people ask me how my boys have not only had the courage to step into life with confidence and joy, but also with such optimism. I'd love to take credit that I am just an ahmaaaaaazing mom. But the reality is that interaction with people like Erik, Patrick, and others is a part of a life lesson. A person can succeed without sight in whatever they choose to do. Some want to climb mountains. Others want to be a stay-at-home parent. The possibilities for thriving as a blind person are endless, just like possibilities for those living with sight are endless.

When I perceived blindness as a burden, I set out to simply survive the challenge with no expectation of greatness for my boys. So I was swallowed up in a journey of despair and devastation. Once I met successful blind adults, my perception of life without sight changed. My mind was open to the endless potential that existed for my sons. That change in perception empowered me to Set Extraordinary Expectations that my sons would indeed find their greatness and fueled me to get tools like Braille and the white cane into their hands. What's been the outcome of these expectations? My boys have played on sighted baseball teams and won championships. They have been in honors programs in top-notch public schools. They participate in more extracurricular activities than my gas tank can keep up with. Michael is in college with big plans for his life ahead, and Mitchell is following closely behind. They have had typical and not-so-typical life struggles. They date girls and go to proms and parties with friends.

Michael is a singer and keyboardist in a rock band. Mitchell has a slew of followers on YouTube. Many of my dreams for them may not come to be. But their lives are about their dreams, not mine. Watching them achieve what they set out to do is a dream come true for me.

Ignite!

In his book *The Talent Code,* Daniel Coyle writes about his theory of how successful people come into their greatness. He makes the case that incredibly high-achieving folks are not born with some kind of supernatural gift. Instead, there are factors involved in their journey that catapult them to their greatness. *Greatness can be learned* is his theory. Mr. Coyle believes all of us, if we follow his formula, can learn to be great. I so agree, simply because I witness it over and over again.

Mr. Coyle believes that once a person has a spark set off in them, it propels them to achieve. Seeing others do what you are interested in doing helps ignite a spark needed to soar to the highest levels. That ignition fuels us to find resources and experts to work through the obstacles that come our way.

People that are achieving their greatness, succeeding without sight, ignited a spark in me and my boys. These role models changed the trajectory of our once very bleak journey. I am honored to introduce you now to thirteen people who inspired me and my children and continue to ignite our journey as we Set Extraordinary Expectations for our lives. My hope is that everyone, blind and sighted, that reads this will be ignited to do the same.

With so much gratitude,
Kristin

Blind Leading the Blind

The Story of Kirk Adams
President & CEO, American Foundation for the Blind

Kirk Adams is currently the President and CEO of the American Foundation for the Blind (AFB). Let me interject a quick lesson here regarding just how major the AFB is by way of a quote from their website: "Founded in 1921, the American Foundation for the Blind has spent nearly a century ensuring that individuals who are blind or visually impaired have access to the information, technology, education, and legal resources they need to live independent and productive lives. From our earliest days, we have amplified the voices of people with vision loss, and have been the engine of advancement and opportunity for every person affected by blindness or vision loss."

Lots of us in the blind community refer to the AFB as "Helen Keller's foundation" because of her involvement with their work for so many years. To say I was honored to meet Kirk is an understatement, and when he agreed to be interviewed for this book, well, let's just say I am glad no one recorded my happy dance! (Cue my daughter's eye roll at just how embarrassing her mother is when she gets really excited.) Why the excitement over meeting a guy who runs an organization? Because they are an incredible resource for the blind community.

To watch and listen to Kirk and me having a conversation would likely make for a great comedy scene in a television show. We couldn't be more opposite. I can talk a topic to death and spin off on hundreds of tangents and sidebars in a matter of minutes—all the while taking bits and pieces of "notes to self" on a napkin. My voice inflection is up, down, and all around as I can get excited, frustrated, mad, sad, and laugh hysterically—all in one five-minute conversation. My passion for my work is definitely boisterous.

Then there is Kirk. While my brain runs a million miles a minute, his brain goes even faster. While I am quickly moving from topic to topic, he is taking notes, looking up information he has to give me, sending someone

> *A lack of independence is one of the biggest frustrations for blind people.*

an email, and checking on where he needs to go next—all the while quietly listening to every word I say and calmly reacting to it all. I can't say hello in under five minutes, but in about five seconds Kirk can give you information that is life changing. Kirk is direct, he is incredibly knowledgeable, and he is so interesting to talk to. His passion for his work is calmly, massively impactful.

We are so incredibly opposite that I nearly fell off my chair when during our first phone call Kirk told me we would have to postpone our interview for the book because he was moving from Seattle to New York City and wouldn't have the time just yet. He said it so casually, like he was telling me he was moving across the street! My mind immediately raced: blind, in a new city, and New York City of all places! "Whoa!" I yelled. "Are you nervous? I'd be nervous! Oh, my gosh, all the stuff to think about! Will you live right in the city? I guess close to the subway? Do you have a mobility instructor lined up?" Unfortunately for Kirk, the firestorm of panicked questions was not just in my mind; they were shooting out of my mouth at record speed! He simply matter-of-factly told me, "Yep, it's going to be an adjustment."

Although the information I collected from Kirk and the other contributors for this book was supposed to impact families new to their blindness journey as well as employers wondering about capabilities of blind workers and others, my eyes were opened to new ideas and tools for my boys with every single interview. You know, I have to admit that there are times on this now eighteen-year journey with raising my children that I pat myself on the back and say: "Way to go, Mom! Your boys are thriving after all that hard work you did!" Then I have a conversation with Kirk that makes me say: "Oh dear God, why hadn't I thought of that?" That's what happened when we did the interview for this book. I was proudly boasting to Kirk about all the activities my oldest son was involved in at his high school and joked about how it would just be so helpful if he could drive himself to everything. Kirk was surprised that Michael wasn't independently getting around town via rides with friends or services such as Uber or Lyft. He calmly coached me through the thought process that if Michael were sighted, he would have so much more independence. A lack of independence is one of the biggest frustrations for blind people. My not allowing Michael, who was completely motivated, to make his own way to and from activities was robbing him of that independence that blind people, and all teenagers, really want! I chalk that one up as Kristin Smedley's Epic Fail #9457. See, I am serious when I say Kirk can give you life-changing information in less than five seconds. Read on and take note of his incredible guidance and the interesting way he met a very special person in his life!

How Kirk Sees It

I wasn't actually born blind. At age five I had cataract surgery, which caused blood vessels in my eyes to hemorrhage, resulting in my retinas detaching. That complication left me blind in both eyes.

I attended a school for the blind for first, second, and third grade. That was the model back when I grew up; it was before the IDEA was passed. (According to the Individuals with Disabilities Education Act [IDEA], your blind or visually impaired child, like any child with a documented disability in the United States, is entitled to educational opportunities in the public school system at no additional cost to you [per www.afb.org].) The model my family followed for me was for a blind child to attend the state residential school until he/she had solid blindness skills to the point where they could go to the public school and be successful. I started public school in fourth grade. We lived in small towns in Oregon and Washington so I was the only blind student in all my schools, even through college and graduate school and being in rural Northwest I didn't know any blind people at all.

My middle school and high school years were tough for me socially, pretty traumatic, actually. Living in small towns you don't have access to public transportation so it was pretty isolating. I wasn't really included in social groups, and although everyone was exploring dating, that was a challenge for me; but then when I went off to college—what a different story! I was able to navigate the college campus and everyone was older and the scene was much more enjoyable for me.

After I was accepted to my small college, Whitman College, I was asked to send a photograph and a little paragraph about myself to the school. There were three hundred incoming freshman, and the school put together a book with everyone's picture and the note about themselves and sent it to all of us before we got to school. This way, we could sort of get to know all the incoming freshman, or at least see who they were. It had an official name but we all called it the "Look Book." My father and my brother went through the book and gave me some "feedback" on all the young ladies in the "Look Book." They determined that a girl by the name of Roslyn Jackson from West Seattle High was the best-looking girl in the book.

So off to freshman year I went, and as I was meeting people the first week of school a young lady introduced herself to me saying, "I am Roslyn Jackson. I went to West Seattle High." We lived in the same dorm, and it turned out she and I had a sociology class together, too. I have to mention here that I was raised by two teachers so I pretty much had obsessive compulsive study habits, which made me a great student and a really great test taker. After the midterm in my sociology class the professor asked me if I would help another student prepare for the next exam. I asked him which student. He told me her name was Roslyn Jackson. I said, "Yes Sir! Yes, I am interested in helping her study!"

I studied with Roslyn for that next exam…and we've been married thirty-one years now.

For the first ten years out of college I was in the municipal securities business. I worked for a firm that underwrote tax-free municipal bond issues in the Seattle area. I sold tax-free municipal bonds over the phone for ten years. Fifty cold calls a day every day. Yep, that kind of job builds character.

That was not my first, second, or any choice for a career. My job search was, unfortunately, typical of a young blind person. I graduated with a degree in economics from a very well-respected college, was Phi Beta Kappa, Cum Laude, and yet I couldn't get a job. So I kept widening my spectrum of what I would be interested in and was offered that job in sales so I took it. I didn't really like it but did it long enough to buy a house and have kids and provide for my family.

I will be blunt: The fact that I could not get employment was directly related to my blindness. There is the "disclose or not disclose" debate that we blind people seeking employment have to deal with. I graduated in 1983 so I was answering jobs posted in the newspaper; there was no internet. I was typing a cover letter and sending a resume. I had great academic credentials and would get plenty of phone interviews. The phone interviews would go really well and I'd get in-person interviews, and then I would arrive at the interview with my white cane and slate and stylus (think blind person's paper and pencil) and confusion would set in. I had lots of interviews but wasn't getting hired. Employers just did not understand how a blind person could get the job done.

I decided to cut out some of those time-wasting episodes and started disclosing in my cover letter that I am blind. In addition, I described how I manage tasks relevant to the job. I said I used Braille and traveled with a white cane. After fully disclosing my blindness and the tools I used to be successful, I wasn't getting any responses at all!

One of the many resumes I sent was to a little brokerage firm, and it turned out that the sales manager had graduated from my same college (Whitman College in Walla Walla). He was also an economics major and had had some of the same professors that I did so he called them to inquire about me. They responded, "Oh yeah, he is a smart, capable guy, and he can do whatever you need." So he called me and scheduled my interview. I got hired. I got a phone and a desk and worked on straight commission. I was thrilled to finally have a job.

Eventually, I was able to move on to a career that was more of interest to me. I worked for the Lighthouse for the Blind of Seattle and then was offered my current position as President and CEO of the American Foundation for the Blind. The job required me to move from Seattle to the big

New York City. So far, so good!

My success in school, careers, and life in general has a lot to do with excelling at blindness skills. Orientation and mobility—the ability to travel independently—is super important. I have to navigate a big city, a large office building, and I fly around the country with my job. Traveling independently is a crucial part of my life.

Braille has been a priority for me, and I believe blind people that read Braille can be more efficient and effective in life. If doing everything electronically and auditorily was so great, then we wouldn't have pencils and paper! You know, sighted people use pencils and pens and paper and take notes and label things and mark things and doodle, and I think it's important that blind people have the same access to that medium. Although I use an electronic Braille notetaker and a Braille display with my PC at the office, I prefer hard copy Braille for reading. (Hard copy Braille is Braille on paper as opposed to an electronic refreshable display.) I have lots of volumes of Braille books from the National Library Service, and I also receive direct circulation Braille magazines.

Technology is another important tool that I use all throughout my day. Some of the technology I use is as simple as a cheap talking alarm clock that wakes me up in the morning and raised dot stickers on appliances in my home. I use a slate and stylus to label my CDs. Most people are familiar with the iPhone; I use that with the built-in voiceover program (voiceover announces everything on the iPhone screen out loud). I also use JAWS screen reading software on my office computer along with an eighty-character Braille display. I still use the Perkins Brailler (which looks similar to an old typewriter) as well as the Braille Sense U thirty-two-character display. Of course, I use the white cane to travel independently. Nowadays, I believe you have to have fluency in technology. It helps me access my environment throughout my day. These skills will become more and more important as we are moving into an age when everything is going to be controlled through some technology interface. If you cannot keep up you are really going to be out in the cold.

With my blindness skills, work ethic, and education, I have had success in my career. I managed the Lighthouse for the Blind in Seattle, and we had 260 blind and deafblind employees. I saw folks that had been sighted but lost their sight and left the workforce. It usually takes approximately eight years to re-enter the workforce; most people never do. The biggest reason for such horrible statistics is that people

> *You know, sighted people use pencils and pens and paper and take notes and label things and mark things and doodle, and I think it's important that blind people have the same access to that medium.*

who lose their sight aren't acquiring blindness skills. Those skills don't just give you the ability to do what you need to do, they also give you the confidence that you can be productive. How do you attain those skills after losing your sight? One very good way is to go to a National Federation of the Blind (NFB) training center like the one in Louisiana. If you can afford it and have the time to do it, then I highly recommend immersing yourself in a residential place like that. It is really hard to acquire blindness skills when you only devote a couple of hours a week to it. For example, if you are getting one hour of Orientation and Mobility instruction each week, it will likely take you five years to develop true mobility skills. At a residential NFB center, within just a few months the training will enable you to be dropped off miles from the center and find your way back using the skills you learn. It is great for skill building and confidence!

For those adults that are raising a blind child, much of this applies as well. In addition, however, you need to let your child do everything that's developmentally appropriate, or everything that you would have your sighted child do. The key is to know the different tools and techniques that allow us to do that developmentally appropriate activity. For example, if a four-year-old sighted child can run around the playground while you sit on the bench, then your four-year-old blind child should do the same with their little cane in their hand.

Parents need to let their blind children fall down and skin their knees and get in fights in the sandbox with the other kids. If the young teens are meeting at the mall to go to a movie together, a blind child needs to know how to do that. Blind teens should also know how to use public transportation or ride services like Uber or Lyft. When kids turn sixteen all of a sudden, sighted kids get driver's licenses and get the first crappy job, and that's where a big divide happens with lots of blind people. They are put in an isolated state where they don't have the same freedom of movement that their sighted classmates do because of driving; they don't get early work experiences and gain traction in the career ladder. Every successful blind person who is employed had a first job, and every sighted person had a first job. The studies show something like sixty percent of young sighted people have paid work by the time they are age 21, but only twenty-nine percent of blind people have paid work by that same age. I think it is really, really important that parents figure out how to get their kid working.

Finally, blind folks should consider consumer groups like the American Council of the Blind and the National Federation of the Blind. I know they are not for everybody but I have seen them be really helpful to people. I advise people to at least check them out and see if one fits. In addition, blind people and caregivers should seek out support networks and sources of information about best practices so you don't have to reinvent the wheel. Also, connect with role models, people who are in professions or careers that you might be interested in, to find out how a blind person does that.

The Bright Side

Blind people tend to be good at risk taking and creative problem solving. One thing I have noticed about myself is that I have a great ability for and lots of experience with putting together and managing teams of people. As a blind kid I really had to manage adults, in a way, insofar as getting things set up so I could do what I needed to do. I had adults assigned to me in grade school and middle school that were doing things like reading tests to me and other things. I had to learn how to effectively communicate with them. Then in college I used readers to access my coursework. I had to interview, hire, and sometimes fire readers and had to manage their schedules. I think that gave me experiences in putting networks and teams together and managing and leading in a way that serves me well in my current work.

Life Is Like a River

The Story of Lonnie Bedwell
Speaker, Author, Blind Adventurer

Lonnie Bedwell has a talent very few people have: The more he talks to me, the calmer I become. Usually, the more I engage in conversation, the more excited I get. Because I have three kids and too much on my plate, my mind goes a mile a minute in a zillion different directions, but not when I talk to Lonnie. Considering the fact that the things we talk about are kayaking, skiing, building things, and all without sight, well, the content is definitely not calming. It's Lonnie. He is sincere, and he is a great storyteller. His humor and calm pace draw you into his funny stories. My favorite story of his regarding his youngest daughter is actually the pivotal moment in his journey of moving from simply surviving blindness to thriving. Lonnie is overflowing with inspiration without even trying, and his fun, kind-hearted nature comes through whether I talk to him on the phone or in person.

I met Lonnie back in 2015 at an event in my hometown of Philadelphia where he was receiving an award for being a great role model for the blind and visually impaired community. Lonnie had just kayaked the Grand Canyon—all 226 miles of it!—and was presented with the prestigious Louis Braille Award from the Associated Services for the Blind of Philadelphia. From the moment he started his acceptance speech, the hundreds of attendees were captivated by his sincerity, his humility, and his humor. Lonnie had my full attention, and I knew right away that this was a person who would have a great impact on the world but, more importantly, on my family.

Lonnie is completely blind. He was not born blind; he had perfect eyesight as a child. As an adult Lonnie was involved in a traumatic accident that left him completely in the dark. I think all will agree it was a miracle he survived that accident. The way I see it, the miracle lies in the fact that he harbored no ill feelings about the accident or his blindness. Blindness certainly did not stop him from, as he says, "being Lonnie."

At the time of our conversation for this book, Lonnie was volunteering his skills as a carpenter and electrician to help build a house in his town. He told me, "I helped frame it, put the roof on, and wired it." He casually added, "I help folks if they need a little something done to their house—toilet repair, roof repair, sink repair, build a deck. It's what I do around here." Huh, no big deal, right? Not to Lonnie, for sure. Lonnie is also an adventurous kayaker and believes life is like a river: Sometimes it's calm, other times it's raging. He compares riding through life like riding a kayak through a long river: When the raging parts get to be too much, you can pull into calmness for a while, but eventually you have to get back in the chaos and move through it.

As you will read, Lonnie's background is quite impressive. I couldn't help but think his experiences leading up to his going blind were just the right experiences he needed to have to come through his accident and "new normal" with his smile and good nature intact. Enjoy Lonnie's adventure!

How Lonnie Sees It

I graduated from college in 1985 with an associate degree in electronics and robotics. I joined the service and was on submarines until I left active duty on May 4, 1994. For nine years I went through drill after drill on those subs, many times with the lights out, to practice how to manage in chaos and in dark chaos. This is a skillset I had no idea I'd eventually need *outside* those submarines. After I left the Navy, I went back to my hometown to join the Army National Guard and helped build and work at a power plant.

For three years, I continued to serve in the National Guard while climbing the ranks to become a supervisor at the power plant. Then, on May 4, 1997, my life changed forever. I went on a hunting excursion with a friend and, in a freak accident, I was shot in the face. Not only did I survive against all odds, I had no permanent damage other than my eyesight. Now I, a father of three young girls, became completely blind as a result of that accident.

I know that my military training helped me get a grip, so to speak, and stay calm through the chaos of what was happening to my eyesight, to my life. Because of my diverse military training, constant drills to develop skills to manage the stress of all kinds of situations, I learned that you have to suppress the chaos to stay focused in your mind. When a crisis or a seemingly insurmountable challenge happens to you, I say to stay as calm as you possibly can so you can react in the best way possible. Doesn't mean the outcome is going to be great, but your odds are better if you stay calm. Once you are calm, you then act. This is a key component of moving from surviving a challenge to thriving in spite of it. You have to take action.

I was in the hospital for a while to recover from the accident. When I had finally gotten home, I was struggling with accepting my situation and was questioning my worth, my value, not only to the world but to my family. I have three daughters—Taylor, Ashley, and Courtney—who were quite young at the time of my accident. I still had to raise them, had to be "Daddy," but I couldn't fathom how I'd manage that when I couldn't even make my way out to my barn and take care of the grass that had grown chest high while I was recuperating. Then along came my five-year-old daughter whom I call "Bug."

I was on the front porch, completely frustrated over the height of the grass. Bug came out and wanted to know what was wrong.

"Daddy, what's wrong?" she asked.

"Nothing, Bug," I replied.

"Now, Daddy," she said, "I know something is wrong."

"I'm frustrated," I said.

> *I continue to raise people's expectations of what people can do without sight. I still mow; I still hunt; I still fish; I still use a chainsaw. I play with the kids and grandkids. I live by myself.*

And then I heard a foot stomp on the porch. Knowing her sassiness, I just knew she likely had one hand on her hip and the other hand pointing at me. She said in a deeper tone,

"Daddy, Why. Are. You. Frustrated?"

I was taken back for a moment and thought, "Wow, I am gettin' called out by a five-year-old!" Then I told Bug of my frustration with the situation with the lawn.

Bug's simple reply, "Daddy, I'll help you."

Help she did! Bug guided me out to the barn and over to the mowing tractor. I climbed on and set her on my lap where she helped me figure out where things were. Once I got my bearings, Bug went up to the house to watch from the porch. I cut the yard and was feeling quite accomplished—until my dad arrived. My dad was shocked to learn that I had taken care of the yard, and he voiced his anger about it. My dad said, "I told you I can help and others are willing to help! You shouldn't be on that mower; it's too dangerous!" But I needed to do things for myself.

I am so fortunate that incident with Bug happened just three months into my challenge. That moment on the porch with her slapped me in the face. Bug made me realize that I had worth and value and purpose; I was wanted and needed and loved. My children didn't care what my eyesight was or was not; they just wanted their daddy. I just needed to be daddy.

That's what I did in the early months and years after blindness arrived. I am a single parent. I taught my daughters how to drive, how to play softball, how to pitch, how to cook—so many things that parents do. Being a parent has nothing to do with eyesight; it has everything to do with your heart, and your soul, and your compassion in caring for your child.

I went full steam ahead into being a typical dad involved in the lives of my children. So typical, in fact, that I even coached their softball teams. It was funny to cause quite a shock in the softball league—teams would arrive for warm-ups to find that a "blind guy" was hitting the ball to the players for fielding practice. I was hitting the balls all over the place, and the girls had to field them! All the while people were whispering in disbelief as clearly this was a sight they didn't expect.

It reminds me of being in Africa very recently where other blind people and I were kayaking the Zambezi River. It stunned the entire area; blind people in Africa are expected to stand on the street corner and beg for money, not soar down a raging river in a kayak!

I continue to raise people's expectations of what people can do without sight. I still mow; I still hunt; I still fish; I still use a chainsaw. I play with the kids and grandkids. I live by myself. I do all regular, everyday stuff. I admit I need help once in a while, but don't we all? Don't we all need a shoulder to cry on, some guidance, some help, once in a while in our lives? I emphasize *once in a while*.

In terms of blind people needing help from sighted people, for sighted people it's pretty simple: Don't assume your help is wanted, simply ask if it is. "May I help you or do you prefer to do it on your own?" It's a simple question with a powerful statement. It tells the person that you believe they are capable. They have worth. They have value. It's a simple statement, huge impact.

It all starts with your mindset. Things will occur in your life that will be a part of you, but they don't have to define you. They don't have to define what you are going to do and who you are going to become. Know that you are a person of worth and value—keep that in your mind. You need to overcome the fear, foolish pride, and pity for yourself. In fact, I define pity as **P**oor **I**nformation **T**o **Y**ourself.

Sure, I guess my advice sounds easy enough for adults to take if they are confronted with a challenge. However, it applies to parents with their children as well. Parents tend to confuse "protect" with "limits" regarding their children, especially blind children. I get the parents' struggle; I honestly do. Parents are wired to protect their children, but not giving your blind child, or any child, the space, tools, and confidence to work things out puts a limit to their potential, their self-worth, and their expectation of purpose.

Imagine you are going along and find yourself stuck behind walls. You can't see or get over, around, under, or through the walls. You're stuck. Someone who has a clear vision of what is on the other side of those walls can put a door in those walls for you. Not only do they put a door there, they open it and either they themselves lead you through it, or they find someone who can lead you through to the other side. On the other side is a full, meaningful, joyful life. If you are the one stuck there, wouldn't you want to walk through to what is waiting for you by yourself? If it is your child stuck behind the wall, wouldn't you want that child to go toward that joyful life? What right do you have to shut and lock the door on him? Are you shutting and locking the door for yourself or for her? Sure, something bad could happen, but something bad can happen to you when you set out into the world each day.

Stop and reflect. Why would you shut the door on your children? Why not let them, *help them*, live the full, happy, joyful, up and down life that we all live. Blind children are no different than the rest of us. They have feelings, emotions, desires, wants, and needs, but they won't be fulfilled if you shut that door.

The Bright Side

I believe first and foremost that the biggest advantage to being blind is that I cannot judge a person by their looks. Period. As much as I want to believe that before the accident I was open-minded, I admit I likely had lots of biases about people based on what they look like. Now, however, I have to get to know who you are a bit before I can make any decision about you. After my accident, a neighbor that I didn't know all that well kept stopping by to lend a hand. One particular day we were on my driveway talking when a friend of mine pulled up. I noticed that as soon as my friend pulled up, the neighbor quickly got in his car and left. My friend warned me, "Lonnie, you want to stay away from him." When I asked why, he went on to describe what the guy looked like, pointing out all the tattoos and other qualities that I guess made him look a certain way that my friend didn't like. I replied, "Do you realize of all my neighbors that gentleman helps me the most? You ought to get to know him and who he is instead of who you think he is."

Another advantage I have had being blind is getting involved in adaptive sports. It has afforded me the opportunity to see the best side of humanity. I have been able to see so much kindness and caring from others. By losing my eyesight, I have been put in a different world I had not been a part of before and have found good, caring people. It is such a blessing.

I am so fortunate to see my purpose in life. I am constantly being told that I make such a difference in so many people's lives. I disagree. I believe I am not the one making a difference; I am just there when others decide they want to make a difference. One guy at my gym thanked me for speaking at his school. He said to me, "I have seen you here before and watch what you do, and I know that you just don't stop. Thank you for that." While I greatly appreciate making those connections, I say, "Don't put me on a pedestal, I am human. I am just Lonnie."

Embrace the Journey

The Story of Diane Berberian
Athlete and Ironman Competitor

Diane Berberian can make talking about a plain cardboard box funny and interesting. To say she treats each day like an adventure is quite the understatement. Although we never had met until recently, from the very first Facebook messages we exchanged I knew I would enjoy our conversations.

A chat with Diane promises at least a few belly laughs. Diane laughs with herself, not at herself, and in so doing helps me see the humor in situations where most of us would only see stress. Diane was one of the first people I invited to be a part of this book. Diane and I were introduced by our mutual friend Val. I wasn't sure how Val and Diane were friends—Val lives in my town in Pennsylvania but Diane lives in Florida. As it turns out, Diane grew up right near where I grew up in the Philadelphia area, and some of the soccer teams she coached were rival teams of the ones I played for.

When I called Diane to talk about my project, we talked for at least thirty minutes before we even got to the main reason for my call! When we did finally get to the point of my call, I rattled off a long-winded explanation of the book and my purpose for creating it. Then I ever so cautiously and caringly asked if she might be interested in contributing the story of her journey with blindness. Once my invite was out of my mouth, I held my breath awaiting her reply. You see, some folks fear a project like this might have a more negative message than a positive one. I get it; I totally do. I know from firsthand experience with my sons that stories like ours and others can easily be told as "Well, bless her heart. Look at this amazing person who, oh my God, has no sight but gets up every day," and that's pretty much it. The fact that a person gets up every day tends to be the amazing story when, in reality, the "amazingness" lies in so, so much more.

Now back to my invitation to Diane. I had my iPhone pressed so tightly against my ear, so nervously awaiting her reply, that my cheek almost disconnected the call. I will never forget her excited reply, "Are you kidding? The last book I was asked to be in was because I was a loser! I love that you want to write about me not being a failure!"

Wait, what? I had only known this woman, this excited, full of life woman, for all of about thirty minutes and that was her reply? I was laughing at the most unexpected response, and I asked Diane to please, please explain! Diane ever so excitedly told me how she had trained for months for her first triathlon competition, but did not do well at all. Later, while she was volunteering at the Great Floridian race, she got to talking to a guy named John Mora about competing and training. She told John the story of her failed first attempt at the triathlon, and he asked if he could include her story in his upcoming book. *Triathlon 101* is about the mistakes people make in training for such a competition and, well, since Diane failed at the event, she was a perfect story for people to learn from!

That's Diane! She gets out there and lives her life, fully, with all heart, all grit, and all the excitement she can find. Diane has competed in over a hundred races, some before and many after losing most of her vision. She celebrates all the good, and learns from all the bad. Interestingly, Diane failed at that first triathlon while she was fully sighted, and then went on to keep competing and achieving when she lost her vision.

With perseverance, humility, and a huge dose of humor, Diane has adopted a mantra of "Embrace the Journey," and the benefits of that attitude are helping her run, swim, and bike her way into the record books for competitions, breaking physical and metaphorical barriers all along the way. Buckle up and enjoy Diane's story!

How Diane Sees It

I lived and worked as a teacher and soccer coach in the Philadelphia area until I was twenty-eight years old. Then I moved to Florida to start a new career in physical therapy. Before the onset of my rare eye disease, I competed in soccer, basketball, volleyball, and softball. To say I was always active is an understatement, but I did have to change activities once my vision changed. I switched to running marathons and moved into triathlons and ironman competitions. I am definitely not one for sitting still!

It wasn't until 2006 when I started losing my central vision. It was not like I woke up one day and had a big void; it was more subtle. I started to notice while driving that I could see the street sign but couldn't make out the letters. I couldn't see the car in front of me, but I'd spot it in my side-view mirror. I would find out about a year later that these odd occurrences were due to macular damage.

I have what is called Idiopathic Juxtafoveal Retinal Telangiectasia (IJT). Here is a definition of my rare eye disease from the National Institutes of Health: **IJT** refers to a group of eye conditions characterized by dilated or twisting blood vessels (telangiectasia) and defective capillaries (tiny blood vessels) near the fovea in the retina. The fovea has the biggest number of special retinal nerve cells, called cones, which enable sharp, daytime vision. In IJT, the telangiectasia cause fluid or crystal buildup and swelling, impairing reflection of light. This results in progressive vision loss.

Currently, my right eye is worse than my left. My vision is down to a 10-degree field, and my retinas are thinning. To me it looks like I am looking through big eyelashes that are constantly in my view.

Despite such a lack of visual field, I can navigate many

> *I like to run alone. I run routes that I have memorized, and I can see enough to follow the grass line next to the sidewalk.*

running paths, swimming lanes, and marathon courses. When I can, I work out alone, and other times with a sighted guide. I believe my brain functions at a higher level and "fills in the blanks" for me. On sunny days I can still ride my bike to the pool for workouts, but cloudy days are tougher for me so a friend will take me there.

I like to run alone. I run routes that I have memorized, and I can see enough to follow the grass line next to the sidewalk. I run the same routes so often that people know me. When I run with someone else I pay attention to what they are doing. I cross the street when they cross, and go up on a curb when they do.

Running with others isn't the only time I follow people closely. I travel a lot to competitions all over the country, and when I fly, I prefer to get off the plane with everyone instead of waiting for the airline to send me assistance. I learned a few years ago that everyone getting off the plane is pretty much heading to baggage claim or transportation so I typically will walk with the crowd and find one person to stay close to in order to find my way. It isn't so challenging as some might think. I have only had one mishap, not actually a mishap. Apparently, I was following someone a little too closely! While deplaning I noticed a woman in front of me with a bright, colorful dress. I thought, "I can see the bright colors, I shall follow her!" Well, I guess I followed too closely for her liking because she got a little snippy with me and thought I was following her in a "weird way." I laughed, explained the situation, and off we went.

I will admit that when my vision problems progressed, I was angry. I work in physical therapy at a nursing home, and I did not want to explain my vision loss to my coworkers and supervisor. I became really good at hiding my visual impairment from everyone, including the clients. If I tripped over something, I would laugh it off as being clumsy. When the eye drops I had to use made my eyes a strange color, I led people to believe I was having cosmetic work done. I couldn't hide it for long, though. One day I leaned in to pick something up and wacked my head on a cabinet and split it open. Another day I was carrying my plate of lunch from the kitchen, through what was supposed to be an empty room, only to find that someone had left a wheelchair in the room. I didn't see it. I tripped over it and sent beans and rice flying all over the floor. I cried. I left work. I went home and applied for disability.

I had a hard time accepting the limitations I was experiencing due to my blindness. As a rehab professional I knew the grief process after such a life-altering experience, but I refused to let myself grieve. As a rehab professional I also knew that I would need time and resources to learn new skills. I denied, however, that I needed any outside help and set out to do the work on my own. "I got this!" I told myself, "Not a problem."

Well, I didn't get anything except more angry and quite isolated. I figured out where everything was in my little condo, but I was living in a bubble of my own little world of existence. Fortunately, I found a group called Achilles International whose mission is to enable people with all types of disabilities to participate in mainstream running events in order to promote personal achievement. I connected with their New York City chapter and learned that they were going to enter a team in the Paratriathlon National Championship in Austin, Texas. I excitedly asked to join the team and was accepted! Not only was this a great event for me to be active and getting out in the world again, but I finally met other people just like me. As I got to know these visually impaired people, I became more comfortable with my vision impairment. It was a pivotal moment in my journey of acceptance of my blindness.

The next step in my journey of acceptance was to get counseling to help me through the stages of grieving my loss. I wasn't grieving the loss of my vision, but a loss of control over the situation. I could not control what was happening to my eyes, and that was very hard for me. I revisit that counselor as I go through stages. It was these counseling sessions where I learned that I would likely go back through certain stages now and again, especially as my vision changes. It is such a relief now to have that knowledge and make sense of what I am feeling. When situations stir things up in me I am able to say to myself, "Oh, okay, I see I am back here again."

I finally was able to move to full acceptance of my blindness when I learned the skills of blindness. Once I learned the skills I needed, the world was open to me again! I got back to my job and back to living a full life! I learned cane and mobility (travel) skills. I learned how to use public transportation to get around town and eventually to go out of town. I realized that the more I was able to do, in terms of getting out and about to places I wanted to go, the more I was comfortable that I would be just fine. I have to say, though, that mobility lessons are not my favorite. I keep asking my instructor if we can do the lesson over the phone but she hasn't given in to that yet!

Technology is really helping me stay social and thrive at work. Using Braille, screen reading software, and screen enlarging software enables me to be independent with paperwork and other tasks in the workplace. My iPhone is especially great for staying connected to my large network of friends around the country via Facebook and Instagram. Social media enables me to expand my world and connect with other blind and visually impaired people. In addition, posting my journey and activities on social media shows the world that I am a real person—blind, active, real.

I have competed in over a hundred races, including five Ironman competitions and four Boston marathons. I run the Boston Marathon with TEAM WITH A VISION from Massachusetts Association for the Blind and Visually Impaired (MABVI). MABVI is an excellent resource for blind and visually impaired people in the Boston area! One day while I was in town, I was even able to shadow a caseworker, a blind caseworker! It was great to travel with him from downtown Boston to Cambridge to meet a new blind client. I watched as the caseworker did all of the intake activities, and I took note of all the support available for the client. I realized how much fuller life would be for blind and visually impaired people in my state of Florida if we had a good support system like they do in Massachusetts!

While running in the Boston Marathons, I got to know the most incredible group of college students: Delta Gamma sorority. Delta Gamma founded Service for Sight, a philanthropy that has been at the heart of the Delta Gamma mission since 1936 when a member who was blind, Ruth Billow, petitioned members to adopt "Aid to the Blind" as the official philanthropy. The Delta Gamma sisters in the Boston area volunteer at the marathon, and they also provide incredible hospitality for the blind competitors! They make dinner for us, give us a place to stay while in town, and provide transportation to and from the race activities. I now seek out Delta Gamma sisters in every city I compete in and have built a strong network in the sorority. I mentor the students regarding life with blindness and how to include blind and visually impaired students in social activities.

As a result of the struggles I had with acceptance of my challenges, I always advise people that are in a similar circumstance to get help right away. It took me a while to seek out blind services and admit I needed intervention. Although I did go through the stages of grief surrounding my loss of control over my vision, I never did have a "why me?" facet of my journey. Anger and frustration, yes, I went through those. But what I came to learn was that the anger and frustration were not about blindness per se, it was about control. This eye disease is not in my control nor are the issues with my vision that fluctuate. I had to learn to manage the feelings around that.

The Bright Side

I have found that since I have lost most of my vision, I finally get to know people without making any judgment at all based on what they look like or what they are wearing. That's something I wish I was able to do from a young age. My friendships are now forged based entirely on who the person is rather than his or her appearance. Not only do I get to know people on a different level, I get to meet a lot of people! Between all of my competitions and the travel and my work, I meet lots of people, and I get to show by example just how "normal" blind people are. The only thing I can't do that I really want to is drive, but I know the technology to make that possible is just around the corner!

I spent quite a bit of time denying and hiding my blindness. Now I welcome my vision changes as an opportunity to recreate myself every few years and have a "new normal." I am not a clear-cut woman! I am unique. Every time I step out and show the world that I am an independent, energetic, intellectual woman, people start to realize that I am not different. I am just Diane.

Raising the Bar

The Story of Michael Corman
Attorney and Stay-at-Home Dad

Michael Corman is smart, talented, and easy to talk to. He has this incredible way about him that every time we talk I learn something new about him and his dynamic life. As you read on, you will likely be as intrigued as I was to learn about Michael's journey from a blind law school student and attorney to adoptive parent and then to second time adoptive parent of a developmentally delayed, blind child from another country!

Michael is descriptive and passionate in his storytelling, but my most favorite part of chatting with him is when he talks about his family. Michael is such a proud dad that you can actually *hear* him smiling on a phone call when he talks about his children, Camille and Jon Paul. Some might say that it is Michael's musical talent that enables him to communicate his feelings more articulately; others might add that being blind gives him an advantage in communicating as well. The way I see it, however, Michael enjoys his role of dad so much that his beaming pride shines right through.

My boys have actually met and played with Michael's son at events with the Blind Sports Organization of Philadelphia. When my guys were younger we traveled many Saturdays to the program that was nearly an hour away in Philadelphia so the boys could learn adapted sports for blind athletes. A great benefit of that was not only did they learn sports skills, they got to meet other children like themselves, which unfortunately does not happen for many blind kids.

Michael left practicing law to become a stay-at-home dad back in 2011 when he and his wife, Faye, adopted their second child. Making the choice to have one parent stay at home is not an easy one for many families, and the job itself isn't an easy one for anyone. Throw in the interesting challenges of blindness (times two!), developmental delays, and language barriers and you've got what most would consider a formula for hardship and frustration. Michael and his wife, however, worked through the barriers to guide their children to thrive, and Michael is blazing a trail to ease the journey for others that follow him.

As you'll read, Michael had a setback in his childhood educational career, and I cannot help but notice that that experience would be a pivotal part in developing his passion for ensuring quality education for blind children. Michael believes that setting the bar higher for blind and visually impaired people is an absolute necessity. I couldn't agree more, and I think you'll feel the same after getting to know Michael a bit here!

How Michael Sees It

When my mother was pregnant with me back in 1963, she contracted German measles. My family did not notice the effects of that illness until months after I was born when they realized I didn't seem to be reacting visually to things. After a trip to a specialist at Wills Eye in Philadelphia, they would find out that I was blind and only able to see light and dark. I actually should have been deaf as well because rubella typically affects the eyes and ears, but I only was affected by blindness.

I grew up in New Jersey but spent my early education years at Overbrook School for the Blind in Pennsylvania.

While Overbrook gave me a good foundation in Braille and daily living skills (how to get dressed, self-care), my family pulled me from that school at the end of my fourth grade year to attend my local elementary school. Unfortunately, my math and reading skills were not up to grade level for the New Jersey public school so I had to repeat that year in the new school. That would later prove to be a very wise decision as I went on to sail through the elementary and middle schools in my hometown and then moved to the private Camden Catholic High School and eventually the prestigious St. Joe's University and ultimately, Rutgers Law School.

I married my incredible wife, Faye, and we started our family by adopting a beautiful baby girl, Camille, from China. I am all smiles when I recall Camille's first days and weeks at home with us in the US. I would come home from work and put Camille in the infant carrier that you wear on your chest, and I would take her out for walks around the neighborhood. As we walked I would talk about the birds and the trees and sing songs to my precious little girl. When Camille was able to walk on her own, she would take my hand as we walked our favorite route through the neighborhood.

I had only ever known blindness so, like others born without sight, adapting is just a "way of life" so to speak. It's innate and not really all that remarkable to people like me that are born this way. For children like Camille that are born into families that have a blind person, adapting to sight loss isn't all that remarkable either; it is just "their normal." I remember one particular incident that demonstrates this beautifully simple but incredibly powerful concept. Camille and I were on one of our walks when she was about two years old. As we were walking together around the neighborhood, we encountered a driveway where there were multiple cars parked and one was blocking the sidewalk, completely blocking the path I

45

had memorized and navigated with my white cane. Without hesitation, Camille, who was holding my hand, simply guided me up the driveway a bit, between cars, around the one in the way, and back to the sidewalk on the other side of the driveway.

I find it remarkable that a two-year-old knows better than most adults: If something is in the way, just find the easiest way to get around it. The bigger part of that moment, however, is that at just two years old Camille anticipated that her Daddy would not know the car was in the way and took the necessary steps to guide me around it. Like I said, for children born into or with a not so typical situation, their resilience isn't necessarily resilience at all, it's just an innate skill, I suppose.

A few years later Faye and I adopted another child, again from China, but this time we took a different, profound route. My wife and I decided to go through a program in which a child with special needs is matched with an adopting family that has "experience" with their needs. Faye and I specifically wanted to adopt a blind child, and we were ecstatic to travel to China to meet Jon Paul and welcome him into our open arms and lives.

We were told that Jon Paul was three years old. When we finally arrived in the room where we'd meet our new son, Jon Paul did not run to greet us, his new parents. He did not talk excitedly about us or ask a million questions like a typical three-year-old. He didn't do anything a typical three-year-old would do. In fact, he couldn't do anything at all.

Jon Paul could not speak Chinese, let alone English. He wasn't potty-trained. He was on the autistic spectrum (something that was not revealed to us earlier). He would do a typical behavior of autistic children called stimming. (Stimming is the repetition of physical movements, sounds, or repetitive movement of objects common in individuals with developmental disabilities, but most prevalent in people with autistic spectrum disorders [per Wikipedia].)

Although the start to my relationship with my son began with challenges I hadn't planned on, Faye and I dove into parenting our little boy the way parents of special needs children do. We made a plan, we gathered resources, and we worked, day in and day out, to achieve goals, big goals, to bring our child up to the level where we knew he could be. For the past five years we have challenged the school district and government agencies to get the tools, resources, and services our son needs to achieve his goals and soar to his greatness, and soar he has. Jon Paul is soaring past all expectations and limits people had on him!

Jon Paul attends the public elementary school in our community, just like all the other kids, but unlike the other kids, Jon Paul is academically above his grade level.

While my wife and I were doing all the not so typical things parents of special needs children have to do to guide

> *He didn't do anything a typical three-year-old would do. In fact, he couldn't do anything at all.*

their child, Jon Paul and I did do one special thing that is typical for my family and typical in lots of families. We took the same "daddy walks" around the neighborhood that I took with my daughter. We talked about the trees and the birds, and as we walked Jon Paul developed his English language skills and his mobility skills, but most importantly, we bonded.

My journey as a blind father has moved into a realm that is quite typical in all households: driving. My wife drives and my daughter will be driving soon so naturally I am interested in getting to know the makes and models of vehicles that my family needs to purchase. I enjoy going to the auto show to explore the different options and new advances. I get a kick out of scaring the hell out of the people that work at the show. Picture their faces as a "blind guy" gets in the driver's seat and asks all kinds of questions, as if I will be driving the car!

I believe a solid education is critical for success for blind children. Actually, "believe" isn't a strong enough word for my passion for this topic. While knowing how to get dressed and cook is important, you aren't going to have anywhere to show up to nicely dressed and well fed if you cannot communicate with people on an intelligent level. I believe Braille and technology skills are crucial to transferring all the knowledge that children acquire in daily life and should be a part of the child's education curriculum.

There are two other areas I am passionate about in terms of raising blind children: social skills and independence. I traveled alone to Switzerland after law school graduation. Trips like that are impossible if you do not have skills in communicating with people and the knowledge of how to get from one place to another. Orientation and Mobility instructors work with blind children and adults to teach them how to navigate street crossings, public transportation, and other tasks. Families that give their blind children diverse experience serve the child well. My parents took me on trips by plane and by ground so that I could understand how different travel systems worked.

I guess that since I have been blind since birth, I am able to look at blindness as a mere inconvenience at times. When I traveled alone to Switzerland, some hotels and street crossings were a little challenging, but the real challenge, the major inconvenience, was the fact that I brought the wrong book to read! I wanted to reference a language notebook but accidently brought a law book on the trip instead. Unfortunately, blind people cannot just head to the bookstore or order on Amazon!

The Bright Side

I think one of the brightest sides to blindness is that you can get through the airport quicker! I tell folks: Just swallow your pride and ask for assistance. In a time when major airports can take a person two to three hours to get from baggage check to boarding, blind passengers definitely have an advantage in being able to bypass some of the long lines; they just need to be willing to receive the assistance instead of attempting to navigate the often overwhelmingly confusing airports alone.

Another wonderful thing I have in my life due to blindness is my guide dog Otis! I am so grateful to The Seeing Eye for connecting us! The Seeing Eye's mission is to enhance the independence, dignity, and self-confidence of people who are blind, through the use of specially trained Seeing Eye dogs. They knew I have kids in the house, and they matched us perfectly. He is a good friend to have.

Guiding Greatness

The Story of Kay Leahy

Mother of Patrick Leahy: Bodybuilder and Capitol Hill Activist

Have you ever been going through something tough and somebody says something to you that literally makes the weight of the world fall off your shoulders? Have you ever met someone in your life and realized that the chance meeting is more than coincidence, so much so that it has to be divine intervention? That happened to me, twice, with Kay Leahy.

In the Introduction to this book I described the nightmare scene I experienced when I first walked into the Leber Congenital Amaurosis (LCA) conference when my first blind son was a baby. It was my first experience in meeting families like mine, families raising blind children. As I said, I was devastated, scared, overwhelmed. But then I experienced Kay's son Patrick give a speech that would impact my journey forever. Pat, then in his early twenties, was the second of two speakers that morning. The speaker before Pat was also a young blind man. He was a medical student that told the audience about his passion for becoming a doctor and all the obstacles he had to overcome to break through what I call the "blind ceiling." His fingers moved swiftly over his Braille notecards; he was a well-spoken guy with a well-planned speech. Then came Pat. He had no notes, no Braille, and no rehearsed speech. Pat was charismatic and funny. He had the audience in stitches listening to stories of his teenage antics, stories that made me forget he was blind. I just saw him as an entertaining person.

I was beyond thrilled to hear the conference organizer announce that Pat's parents were in the audience and they had agreed to do a question and answer session with the parents of blind children in attendance. I think I may have pushed and shoved people out of my way to get a seat in the small area where Kay and her husband were addressing people. The floor was open to ask anything regarding raising a successful blind child. There were so many questions from parents like me that were starving for information about how to raise a blind child to grow up to be as wonderfully successful as Pat. There were questions about school and siblings and technology and Braille and college. I couldn't think ahead to college. I couldn't even think ahead to preschool. It was too overwhelming. I had one burning question that was gnawing at me, day in and day out, and I needed to hear Kay's answer. I finally had an opportunity. I nervously choked back my tears as I asked her: "When did you stop crying every single day?" She looked at me with a look not many people understand. She looked at my heart with her heart. She *knew*. She knew the devastation I was feeling. She knew the pit of sadness I was in. She knew how hard it seemed to climb out. She walked this path before I did. She knew. Kay very graciously, seriously, and lovingly said to me, "One day you will realize that you didn't cry at all that day. I can't tell you when it will come; but trust me, the day will come. Then you will have a couple of days in a row without tears, and then a whole week. Eventually, you will not feel this deep sadness and fear that you have today. You'll get there."

Then she said the most amazing thing to me. She said, "Look at my son and how successful, wonderful, and comfortable he is. I still have a day every now and again when I am sad. It's okay. It happens, and then it passes."

You know what? She was exactly right. That is exactly what happened and still happens. I do get triggers every now and again, like when friends post their newly licensed teen drivers' pictures on Facebook. However, Kay was exactly right: The sadness lasts only for a bit and passes as I shift my focus back to all the joy and blessings my children are to this world.

I don't see it as a coincidence that Kay and Pat and I were at that conference on that day. Nor do I see it as a coincidence that ten years later I was in a meeting at my second blind son, Mitchell's, school creating the Individualized Education Plan for his fourth grade year. Tara, the teacher he had been assigned, told me she had some experience with blindness; her brother-in-law is blind. She told me he lives in Washington, DC. She told me that he also has LCA. Then I realized what this fourth grade teacher's last name is: Leahy. It turns out my Mitchell's teacher is the sister-in-law of Patrick and the daughter-in-law of Kay. Moments like that happen on my journey all the time.

How Kay Sees It

My son Patrick (Pat) is forty-three years old and has been visually impaired since birth due to Leber Congenital Amaurosis (LCA). He lives in the Washington, DC, metro area. He has worked for several Congressmen and Senators and now is a Senior Advisor for the Federal Election Committee. Pat has a guide dog named Galahad but he is also skilled at using the long white cane to navigate.

Although there are now more than twenty genes identified that cause LCA, we do not know the gene that is affecting Pat. We did not know right away that Pat had LCA; it was a guessing game for a while. I could tell when Pat was three or four months old that he was not tracking things like his older brother did. I got suspicious that something wasn't quite right and took him to an ophthalmologist who told me Pat was completely blind and likely had intellectual limitations as well due to a virus I contracted during my pregnancy. My husband's knees buckled at the news.

For the next year and a half we had to "wait and see" how he developed. Pat showed us that developmentally he was fine, he just couldn't see much. One thing, in particular, that we noticed was that Pat responded to things that were in his peripheral view; he had some vision there! When Pat was three years old we took him to a new doctor who did not agree with the "virus theory" and wanted to investigate further. The Electroretinogram (ERG) had just been made available so the doctor wanted to try it to get a better understanding of what was going on with Pat. An Electroretinogram is an eye test used to detect abnormal function of the retina (per Medicine.net). To conduct the test, the doctor puts what looks like a contact lens on the patient's eyes and uses clamps to hold the eyelids open. Then the "lenses" measure the responses the eyes make to the visuals the patient is shown. As you can imagine, Pat hated the test and went wild in the exam room. The staff sedated him with special medication, but he had a reaction to the medicine. We did not go any further with that test.

Luckily, about a year later, we were sent to Johns Hopkins to see Dr. Irene Maumenee, a world-renowned expert in rare eye diseases including LCA. Dr. Maumenee performed an exam under anesthesia, a very good way to see what was happening in Pat's retina without upsetting Pat. She got a good look at Pat's retina and determined he had LCA.

When Pat was diagnosed with LCA all those years ago, there was no hope at all for a cure so I focused all of my energy on helping Pat to be all he could be. Nowadays, there is so much hope for a cure that I want to caution parents to be sure to still spend time getting their blind child the tools they need to be successful without sight. I believe you have to have a balance; you can put your hope in research, but you also must put in the time with your child. It takes quite a bit of time to guide a young blind child and to advocate for them.

Since I didn't know any successful blind people, I had to figure things out as we went along. Pat had a little bit of sight when he was young, and his teachers wanted him to try to use his sight as opposed to learning blindness skills. I had a huge argument with the school because I wanted him to learn Braille. We had no idea what the future would bring for Pat; we didn't know if his minimal vision would deteriorate. I wanted him to be prepared in case it did. The staff were upset that I was requesting Braille and would not listen to my request. I just couldn't understand why they would fight me on it. I mean, they offered classes in other languages so why not another form of literacy like Braille? The school actually had a psychologist from a school for the blind call me and try to talk me out of fighting for Braille! I shared with that person my view about how Patrick needed to have tools in his toolbox that would prepare him just in case his vision declined. The psychologist ended up agreeing with me so Braille was added to Patrick's IEP (Individualized Education Plan).

Now, after all the advocacy and follow-through to teach Patrick Braille, he still tried to use his minimal vision to see things on a closed circuit tv (CCTV). He would put his nose to the screen of that device to look at one inch high print. He did that for a while—until he realized that it was just slowing him down in the classroom. Once Patrick got it in his head that there were more efficient ways to do things, it got much easier. All of the work to get the right tools was worth it because Pat's vision faded in college. Since he did not learn Braille very early on and was encouraged to use his minimal vision, his Braille skills are not superb. The funny thing is he now mentors a young blind child that uses Braille. Pat said to me: "Mom, he is getting so good at Braille that he is moving beyond my skill level!" Patrick has figured out how to combine his skills—Braille, technology—to accomplish what he wants to do.

Social life in Pat's middle school and high school years was tough. Many kids were kind but not all were. Nobody taught the other children about how a person lives without sight. Pat is a person, a person that happens to be blind. The teenagers did not get that. College was a whole different ball game. Pat went to a state university, Millersville University. They had a great disability services department, more than the average services most schools had. It was a diverse campus so it wasn't just one group of people. There

> *Once Patrick got it in his head that there were more efficient ways to do things, it got much easier.*

were people from different economic, ethnic, and cultural backgrounds. With diversity and differences already "built in" combined with the students being older and more mature in college, Pat was seen as a person, not a blind person. He was even elected president of the student body in his senior year. He thrived in that environment.

Pat wanted to be a meteorologist. I did some research and found out that a blind student had gone through the meteorology program at Penn State. So we knew that it was possible for Pat to succeed in that major at his school. The Meteorology department staff at Millersville were wonderful. But by the end of freshmen year Pat decided that he loved meteorology, but not enough to make it his career. He switched majors to political science and never looked back.

Pat also found a passion for weightlifting and bodybuilding. For many years he was a competitive bodybuilder. Pat was even featured on The Today Show for his bodybuilding success! He still loves going to the gym. It is a big stress relief for him. Pat also enjoyed other sports like downhill skiing.

Extracurricular activities are important for blind children, but they also need to be proficient in computer, Braille, and mobility skills. I have witnessed how being proficient in each of these areas, at or above the level of the other children, makes the difference for blind children.

In my opinion, getting mobility training as soon as possible is essential. Pat navigates the public transportation system to get into work every day with his guide dog. He chose a wonderful home to live in but he needs to take two different metros to get into work. He navigates that just fine, thanks to his mobility skills. He uses Uber to get around as well.

The Bright Side

When Pat was young it was great to go to Disney World and get wonderful access to the rides and all, but the "brighter" side I see to blindness is that Pat really knows how to listen to people. He does not get distracted by what they look like or what they are doing. He can hear things in a person's voice that the rest of us don't pick up on. For example, he dated a girl years ago that was a lovely person, but Pat could hear an attitude he didn't care for in the way she interacted with others. Pat said she was very nice but he noticed how critical she was in the way she said things, and that was something I did not pick up on. He can usually recognize things about an individual right away where it would take me ten times of interacting with her to get it!

Another bright side I see that many people might not realize is the benefit that blindness had on our entire family. Pat's older brother, Bill Jr., learned from a young age that our family was a team and we needed to be there for each other. Bill Jr. did just that for his brother: He was there for him. Pat knew he had a brother that cared about him. Pat's dad, Bill, often taught me about letting go even in some challenging moments with Pat. Our family came together as a team.

Parents of blind children should know that you are going to get stuck in the loss for a while, and that's okay. Finding out your child is blind is a very difficult loss, and you feel for the child. Fear sets in as you worry about being capable of raising the child. It takes time to process that, and that's okay. I was stuck in the loss, too. I had lost both of my parents by my teenage years. It was a devastating time for me, but I worked really hard to climb the ladder out of the loss and out of that place I was stuck in. I went to nursing school, got married, and had my first child. My life was wonderful. Then Pat was born, and I found out he was blind. It was like somebody came along and just pushed the ladder over with me on it. I was so afraid: How am I going to do this? Am I going to be able to do this? Of course, I just loved my child and hated that this happened, and for three and a half years I thought his blindness was caused by me—that did not help matters! I was hard on myself for a couple of years, but when I found out the cause was due to genetics I thought, "Oh my gosh, I couldn't have done anything; it just happened." That did make it a little easier to deal with Pat's challenging circumstance. I then moved forward and got my son the tools he needed and watched him grow and become a fine young man.

The best start a family can have in raising a blind child to be all he or she can be actually begins with the doctor that diagnoses the child. I think it would make such a difference if a doctor would say, "I know learning that your child is blind is hard for you, but with the right education, programs, and tools, they are going to do just fine and live a full life." In addition, connecting with positive parents of blind children and hearing their real-life stories of successes and challenges is a much needed resource for affected families. If a family starts out on a positive note with the doctor, and then has support from parents that have walked their walk, what a difference it will make for them! Most importantly, the child will benefit and become a capable adult who will bring many fine qualities to society.

Walk by Faith, Not by Sight

The Story of Scott MacIntyre

Musician, American Idol Finalist

My family and I have been so fortunate to experience Scott through his gift of music. Scott's dream since he was a very young child was to perform on stage and affect a large crowd, and I was blessed to experience him do that and one better: I got to watch my children witness their idol on stage.

When you are a young person you tend to have role models, people you aspire to be. For many of us, those role models are accessible by way of TV or movies. My daughter is a soccer junkie and watches videos of Mia Hamm, Carli Lloyd, and Abby Wambach over and over. She tunes in to US Women's National Team games every time they are on TV and watches and cheers for the women that she hopes to be one day.

My younger son, Mitchell, wants to be a weather anchor when he grows up so you can usually find him watching his role model, Sam Champion, on The Weather Channel. My older son, Michael, follows his favorite musicians and dreams of selling out stadiums like his heroes Bruce Springsteen and Bon Jovi.

My sons are blind, and finding someone like them on TV was pretty much nonexistent. Even with diverse programming and the onslaught of reality TV shows, there were still no characters, no representation of blind people, in mainstream media that my boys could relate to or be inspired by. Enter Scott MacIntyre. In 2009 my boys were just nine and six years old. That year Scott's participation on *American Idol*, the show that dominated pop culture, week after week opened up possibilities for my guys, and he gave the world a glimpse of the fact that blind people are people and can run in the same circles and grace the same stages as sighted people.

Scott's time on the *American Idol* stage week after week blew open people's perceptions of blindness. Sure, the world had been exposed to and blessed by the musical gifts of blind people like Stevie Wonder and Ray Charles, but Scott was *live*. He was dancing in the choreographed numbers, and he blended right in with all the sighted contestants. Although Scott was working to stand out as a star, my family cheered as he looked just like everyone else; his blindness didn't make him different.

The impact Scott had on our family was bigger than just opening a possibility of being able to compete on the biggest talent stage. Scott also opened Michael's mind to the fact that he could handle a ton of choreography involved in his middle school production of *Thirteen the Musical*. He showed Mitchell that charm and wit during live interviews goes a long way in winning people's affection and breaking down social barriers that often exist between blind and sighted people. He showed all of us that a sense of humor, combined with being comfortable with yourself, sets the stage for others to be comfortable, too. I think you'll find Scott to be just as "normal" and as fascinating as my children and I do!

How Scott Sees It

I was born almost completely blind and see about two degrees of tunnel vision. That field of vision is about the size of the mouse cursor on a computer screen. The cause of my blindness is unknown.

I live in Tennessee with my wife, Christina, and our son, Christian. I currently work in the entertainment industry as a recording artist, songwriter, inspirational speaker, author, and music producer. I use a screen-reader every day for email, web browsing, typing out song lyrics, and many other tasks. I also use several handheld magnification devices to read printed material like business cards or business documents.

When people ask me what I consider a crucial skill for blind people to perfect I say: Learn to ask for help. It sounds simple, but no matter how independent we are and how accessible the world is, there will be times when we get stuck. There's nothing wrong with being vulnerable. Also I've always tried to connect with sighted people and make them feel comfortable around me, and one way I do that is to turn my face in the direction of the person who is talking to me. A blind person might naturally turn his or her ear toward the speaker, but I learned to turn my face toward the person with whom I am speaking even though I may not be able to see that person. I know it helps him or her to know I'm listening.

For those parents that are raising blind children: Always encourage your blind child to try new things— within reason! Don't be afraid to allow him or her to take risks. Before I believed in myself, my parents believed in me, and they created safe situations in which I could test my limits and discover what I could do and what I couldn't do. As a result, I have skied, body-surfed, rock-climbed, and realized my dream of a career in music.

Most of us have probably heard the phrase, "seeing is believing." Although there is nothing inherently wrong with this idea, it teaches us to wait for results before taking action. I believe there are talented, intelligent, driven people all over the world who have dreams and ambitions, but very few people reach for their goals and dreams without first being able to "see" that they are realistic. In reality, however, people are able to accomplish much more than they may realize, and believing that something is possible and committing to that idea is the first step to achieving results. In other words, contrary to popular thought, perhaps believing is seeing.

Today people all over the world know me as the first person with a disability to become a finalist on *American Idol*. They know me as a TV personality or a singer-songwriter and pianist with an inspirational story, but very few can imagine the obstacles I had to overcome in order to be where I am now.

> *Learn to ask for help. It sounds simple, but no matter how independent we are and how accessible the world is, there will be times when we get stuck.*

I have been blind since birth, and consequently I was drawn to the world of music and sound from the very beginning. I clearly remember lying in bed at night as a kid and dreaming about someday performing in arenas and what that would be like. I didn't know how to get there, and I certainly didn't have a clue yet about what challenges I would face as a blind musician competing in the very visual entertainment business. However, I could imagine it, and that was enough to get me started on the right path.

I began playing piano by ear at the age of three, and soon after began classical piano training. It was always a learning experience for every new piano teacher I worked with because none of them had ever taught a blind pianist before. In a sense, my parents, my piano teacher, and I were figuring it out as we went along, discovering what worked for me and what didn't. Obviously, I was never able to read sheet music due to my blindness so my teacher would record the music for me on a tape, each hand separately; then I would listen to the tape, learning the left hand, then the right hand, and eventually putting them together.

One of my earliest teachers taught me a lot about excelling at the piano and also in life. At the time when I would play a piano piece that required me to move quickly from one note on the keyboard to another note extremely far away from the first, I would use my fingers to feel my way across the dozens of keys in between until I found the note I needed to play. One day, my teacher said, "Scott, I don't want you to feel all those keys anymore. I want you to play the first note, then lift your hand off the keyboard in an arcing motion, and come down right on that other note! You don't need to feel your way. You just need to *know* exactly where that note is."

He was asking me to take a leap of faith, to do something I had never done before, not to mention it was way outside my comfort zone. Nonetheless, he insisted that I could do it. So I gave it a try. I lifted my hand off the keyboard, hoped for the best, and completely missed my target! I wasn't even close, but I didn't stop there—I could understand in my mind what he wanted me to do, and I kept trying. Eventually, I hit the right note, and before long I was doing it every time. I carried that confidence with me for the rest of my life, and every time I overcame a new obstacle, I found more confidence to overcome the next. It was the same confidence that allowed me to enter college at fourteen years old, graduate at age nineteen, *summa cum laude*, become a Marshall and Fulbright scholar, and live independently as a person with a disability overseas in London, England. The pattern was always the same. Before I succeeded, I had to be able to see it happening in my mind.

In 2008, I was at home watching *American Idol* with my family. Many people had asked me if I would ever consider auditioning for the hit Fox TV show, but I had never felt it was the right place for me since at the time the contestants only sang and were not allowed to play an instrument. All that was about to change. Suddenly, a grand piano was wheeled out on stage, and one of the contestants sat down to play and sing. I thought to myself, "If only I could be in her shoes, playing and singing for millions of people..." That was all I needed. I didn't spend any time wondering how in the world a person like me with a disability would fit in on the world's biggest reality show, or how I would be able to participate in the heavily choreographed group songs, or how I could connect with TV viewers when I couldn't even see the cameras. All I knew was that my dream was to sing and play for millions of people, and now *American Idol* was a viable option for making that happen.

The *Idol* producers had never worked with a person with a disability before so there were plenty of obstacles to face throughout my time on the show. In every case, I made an effort to rise to the occasion, and consequently they were willing to venture into uncharted territory with me, breaking barriers and changing paradigms every step of the way. No one would have ever thought that a blind individual could or should dance and sing on the *Idol* stage in front of thirty million viewers until they witnessed me doing exactly that. There was no precedent to show me the way, only my belief that it could be done.

The Bright Side

There are three facets of my life that directly benefited due to my disability: my abilities in music, memorization, and trusting others. I was drawn to the world of sound, which fostered my interest in and passion for music. I developed a strong memory since I had to memorize my surroundings, people's voices, and the music I learned. Trust was required of me when I had others guide me around or when I relied on another's word concerning things I couldn't see for myself.

In my short life, I have released numerous CDs (including *Lighthouse,* which brought "Remarkable" to #1 on the Christian Radio Chart); headlined concerts in the US, Canada, Mexico, Japan, and Vietnam; performed with pop icons like Alice Cooper, The Band Perry, and Jonas Brothers; and toured in arenas across North America—just like I had imagined as a kid.

I never expected all this to happen or assumed it would, but I knew beyond the shadow of a doubt that it was possible. This belief kept me focused on my goals throughout the entire journey there. Sometimes the hardest part is getting started, but the only way we can truly know our limitations is to test them. Goethe put it this way: "Whatever you can do, or dream you can, begin it! Boldness has genius, power, and magic in it. Begin it now."

Music to My Eyes

The Story of Bill McCann
Founder, Dancing Dots

Bill and I have something in common: We are rarely at a loss for words! Our conversations tend to be long and entertaining, always entertaining. So the fact that the way we met is a long story, well, that is just as it should be in our case. I connected with Bill's company, Dancing Dots, through a family friend while I was on vacation one summer a few years ago. That meeting involves a long "who's who" story in the family tree so I will spare you some time and attention span: I met Bill's business partner, Albert, while our families were "down the shore," as we say in my town (people outside the Philadelphia area say "at the beach"). I chatted with Albert and his family about my boys and blindness, and then Albert shared information about his work with a company called Dancing Dots. Bill McCann founded Dancing Dots in 1992 to develop and adapt music technology for the blind. My oldest blind son, Michael, was just getting interested in music when I met Albert so the information about this company was quite interesting to me. Albert eventually connected me to Bill to help me get Braille music books into Michael's elementary school music program.

Not too long thereafter, Michael started getting very interested in creating music with his digital piano and his computer, something his good friend Rocco Fioretnino was heavily involved in. Rocco is a gifted musician who is also blind (he's like mega-gifted; check him out at www.musicbyrocco.com). He had become one of Michael's closest friends and our mentor for all things blindness related. Rocco recommended some starting points for digital music, and Bill helped steer Michael and me through the programs Michael would need to get started exploring and composing.

I could not believe the world that Dancing Dots opened up for my son. He was always heavily involved in sports and school activities, and it was wonderful to watch him enjoying life, but there was something about music and Michael. When Michael was able to create incredible pieces of music with his computer and a simple digital piano, a whole new side of him opened up and shined. Dancing Dots is *that* fantastic! Bill helped us build a perfect system for Michael to be able to work in a program called SONAR. Combined with their CakeTalking scripts, SONAR became fully accessible for him to independently create music tracks. I don't want to completely geek out here with all the technical stuff it can do, and I don't even understand all of it anyway, but let's just say that this program rocks!

Over the years I have bumped into Bill at conferences and meetings where we are both presenters, and we always have great conversations talking about a zillion different things. The day that Michael got to meet Bill in person, however, was priceless. Both Bill and Michael were honored at the Pennsylvania State Capitol for being role models for the blind. After the ceremony I introduced Michael to Bill. They both excitedly talked about all their favorite music programs and iPhone features, and on and on and on they went! Talk about two peas in a pod! I made my way around the event and talked to every single person there while those two chatted up a storm. Michael was on cloud nine to talk with someone as knowledgeable and easygoing as Bill, and Bill seemed just as enthralled.

As you'll read in Bill's story, he did not always have the opportunity to follow his music passion. Like so many of us, his passion got put on the back burner to be able to pay the bills, but I am sure so many others that have been impacted by Bill's work will agree: Thank goodness life worked out for Bill to pursue a career in music!

How Bill Sees It

I am number seven in birth order of a family of eight kids. My mother had German measles during her pregnancy with me, and she would find out when I was about a year old that it resulted in my having Congenital Glaucoma. (Glaucoma is a rare condition that may be inherited, caused by incorrect development of the eye's drainage system before birth. This leads to increased intraocular pressure, which, in turn, damages the optic nerve [per Glaucoma Research Foundation].)

When I was a year old my Mom just knew something was not right with my eyesight. She noticed that being in the sunshine was painful for me; every time I went out into the sun, I cried, and I sneezed. (I swear to this day I think about the sun and I sneeze!) By the time I was six years old I had more than nineteen surgeries to relieve the pressure that kept building up in my eyes. Regardless of all the surgeries, I still lost all of my usable vision by the time I was six years old.

At the time I had my final surgery and lost all of my sight, I only wanted one thing for Christmas: a bicycle. It seemed like all the kids had one, and I wanted one, too. On Christmas morning there it was, my very own bicycle! My parents did not say, "Well, you can't see anymore, and we are not sure if this is a good idea." They just stepped aside and let me enjoy the gift I wanted so much. When the snow melted, my dad took me outside to ride it. I initially used the training wheels but eventually was able to ride without them. I learned how to ride it around our driveway. I'd go pretty slowly, and I could hear if there was a car parked and I could go around the car. After a while I was able to ride on our sidewalk, up and down the street. I knew every bump in the sidewalk. I had a lot of fun riding for as long as I could. When I got a little older and my best friend wanted to ride through the entire neighborhood, I would pedal the bike while he sat on the crossbars to steer and be my eyes! We would ride around the entire neighborhood and had so much fun.

The driveway at my childhood home was essentially a double wide driveway; ours was right next to our next door neighbor's so we had two driveways side by side to play on. Everyone in the neighborhood came over to play, so much so that my mom called it the neighborhood playground. I was involved in all the activities; we just made up accommodations as we went. For example, in kick ball, I would kick the ball and someone else would run the bases. We tweaked each game a little, and I was completely involved. As I got older, though, the competition on our double driveway got more serious so I wasn't able to join in anymore. Actually, I kind of liked it better. I love music so I started listening to more music and took lessons. While kickball games were getting more serious on the driveway, I was inside getting serious about my passion for music. I started playing the trumpet and devoted my free time to building my skills with that instrument.

From kindergarten through eighth grade, I attended St. Lucy's Day School for the Blind in Philadelphia. Since their founding in 1955, their "mainstreaming" model was for the blind students to attend some classes with all the blind students and then go across the street to the "regular" school and take more and more classes with sighted kids. I eventually realized my dream that I worked hard for: to go to the local high school, Monsignor Bonner, with my brothers. It was in high school that blindness kind of snuck up on me. Let me explain. Things are quite different now in terms of mobility training for blind kids. Nowadays kids are getting their white canes at two or three years old. I never had that; I was walking *and* biking around my neighborhood without a white cane. At age fourteen, when I started at Monsignor Bonner, they arranged for a mobility teacher to teach me about how to use the cane. Well, my reaction was: "I don't need that!" You see, in my little world I could get around just fine, but my teachers and my family knew I would eventually need to leave my little world and navigate a much bigger one. I reluctantly started my lessons, and I realized I did not feel comfortable at all. Now people would know; they would know that I couldn't see. I had been enjoying the fact that I could walk around and bike around and people didn't know that I was blind. That somehow made me feel more included. I didn't stick out, but when I had the cane in my hand, I realized the pretending is over. Everybody knows. I hated it. It certainly didn't help to hear people say "what a shame" when they would see me with the cane. I bought into that shame for a while, but over time I realized the independence the cane gave me. I finally said to myself, "Well, I can't see. It's not a shame. It's me. It's part of the package that I am, and with this cane I can go places!"

Go places I did, starting with music lessons. While in high school I switched from playing the trumpet to the flute. I had to travel a few miles to Overbrook School for the Blind to take flute lessons. So afterschool I would take a city bus, independently, to Overbrook to meet the music director for lessons. Interestingly, it was at Overbrook that I had an encounter with a really rude, socially inept blind person. I was walking through the big rotunda, tapping my cane as I moved through the building. Suddenly, someone came charging through the space and knocked into me, hard. I was trying to catch my breath and get my bearings when the person yelled, "Who are you?" Turns out it was another blind student, and he was barreling through the building with no cane in hand. I thought to myself, "Now why would a blind person, why would *anyone,* bang into someone and then yell at them?" I was thankful that my family had taught my siblings and me better social skills!

My mobility skills have been such a great asset. I have independently traveled to and walked around cities like Philadelphia, New York, Los Angeles, London, Madrid, and Warsaw. A note to all especially young readers: People, like parents and teachers, often actually know what they're talking about when they insist that you learn a particular skill or subject area.

After graduating high school and completing my bachelor's degree in trumpet performance, I couldn't seem

> It certainly didn't help to hear people say "what a shame" when they would see me with the cane. I bought into that shame for a while, but over time I realized the independence the cane gave me.

to find full-time music work so I decided to enroll in a program at the University of Pennsylvania to learn how to program computers. The training program was in partnership with local companies like Sunoco and included a two-month unpaid internship, which I served with that company. The internship went well, and Sunoco offered me a full-time job. It was difficult for me to give up my dream of a music career for a desk job, but I had to take the opportunity to earn a salary and figure out music later. I worked for ten years as a programmer for Sunoco, but I became increasingly bored with my work. I loved that I was able to provide for my family but, especially during the last few years there, I would start work at, say, 7:30 a.m., and after what felt like five hours had passed, it was only 8:30 a.m.! All the while I kept thinking about a way to fit my passion for music into my life. An opportunity finally came my way.

Ever since my college days, I had been dreaming of an idea to create software that would turn print music into Braille music. In late 1991, Sunoco was offering severance packages for people to voluntarily leave the company! I discussed the possibility of pursuing my idea full time with my wife, Mary Ann, and she was all in for it. She knew how unhappy I was with my job, and although we were expecting our second child and there were no guarantees that this idea would work out successfully, she told me to go for it. What a gift that was! In the end, I ended up making more money than I did at Sunoco and had so much fun and helped a lot of people all over the world.

It wasn't an easy transition, though. I had a growing family and now was launching a new business so I filled our financial gap by getting gigs with my band and some part-time contracts teaching adults and children how to program.

After leaving Sunoco, I applied to Pennsylvania's Ben Franklin Partnership for start-up funding. That six-month grant led me to a federally funded program called Small Business Innovation Research. I proposed my idea, and our new company, Dancing Dots, was awarded funds from the US Department of Education to create a prototype of the software.

The prototype read a music file called a MIDI file. It determined what the notes were and converted them to Braille characters that I could send to a Braille printer or Braille display so a blind person could "see" the music.

Based on the prototype, the US Department of Education funded the development of the next stage of the program, which allowed me to hire my business partner, Albert, who has stayed with me on this incredible journey ever since. People who read Braille music loved our product, and people who transcribed Braille music loved it because if you can see the print music and use a computer, you can function as the transcriber. Our software is kind of like a word processor for print music notation, combined with a tool to automatically convert that information into the Braille music system. If you enter music into the program, it appears on the screen as standard staff notation. When you are happy with the on-screen score, you can pass it to the GOODFEEL® component, which automatically converts it to the equivalent Braille music. Now a school band director or a friend that can read print music can transcribe a blind student's music quickly without having to be a Braille music expert. Before this program, sheet music had to be mailed off to a nice volunteer somewhere to be transcribed, and the blind student had no guarantee that it would be returned in time for the rehearsal, concert, or competition.

Automating Braille music transcription was our first step. Next, we moved into making audio production software accessible for blind musicians. We teamed up with a developer, David Pinto, who had made some scripts for JAWS for Windows (a screen reader program) to work with a program called SONAR, which is a mainstream program that converts your PC into a recording studio. David wrote some really nice scripts we called CakeTalking for SONAR that made it simple for people who couldn't see the screen to use the program.

More recently, we added features to our own software to make our music notation program friendly to people with low vision. The Lime Lighter component magnifies the print music on screen and allows you to scroll the music using a wireless pedal, keeping your hands free to play your instrument. We also publish books on learning Braille music and do a lot of training and consulting in the area of music and the visually impaired. I like to say we serve a niche market but it is a big need. We have customers for our software now in more than fifty countries.

In my journey I have come to realize that there is a reason God made everyone different. It would be so boring if we were all the same. We are different so that we can be interdependent: I can do something for you, you can do something for me. Of course, we should be as independent as possible; we shouldn't be just waiting for other people to do stuff for us that we could do ourselves. When you get to a point where you are so absolute and think "I don't need anybody," that is just not healthy. When I was younger, I was independent, which served me well, but as I got older, I realized the goal wasn't so much independence as interdependence. When I was young, I wouldn't let anyone help me cross the street, but now there are times when I do accept the offers. I like to consider that a person offering to help may not have ever met a blind person, or a person with a disability, and my moment with them can be a big moment. They may feel great for helping me cross a street, but what an impact I can have on them when I then tell them I can manage to my destination on my own from there. A quick interaction like that can go a long way in educating the general public about how capable blind people are. I get to talk with someone outside of my own world for a moment and our worlds intersect.

My wife and I have five children, and they are all individuals. Blind kids are no different. One blind child is not necessarily like every other blind child. There are certain things in common, but it's important to see them as individuals and try and connect them with what they love, what they are good at, and what interests them. Blind children need to be guided, not smothered! There is no checklist for how you do that. When you have a one-year-old who wants to go out the door by themselves, you tell them you can't let them do that. Then one day when they are older and want to do it you say, "Yeah, that's okay; go ahead." When that day is there is no telling, but as a parent you have to be tuned into that. When is the right time? For one kid it is different than another. That's the art of being a parent. There is no set answer. There is no formula. You have to be in tune. You know, I was child number seven of eight, and the only blind child in my family. My parents didn't have time to worry about me so much. Oh, if they knew some of the stuff I did! I remember I used to climb this tree in front of my house, and I'd climb it and be higher than my house. It was a huge old maple tree. I would just sit up there in the breeze. Someone in the family would call me, "dinner time," and I'd just sit up there. One time, I guess it was in the Fall and the leaves had fallen, my father saw me up in the tree and yelled, "What are you doing?! Get out of that tree!"

I knew I had great parents, but now I know that even more as a parent myself. I know you have to let your child go by degrees, even if you sometimes feel like you just aren't ready. It's a natural and necessary process that is not usually completely comfortable for all involved.

The Bright Side

I know that blind folks "qualify" for the handicapped placard for the car, but my wife and I never got one of those. I can walk just fine and don't need it, but when it's pouring rain and we have to park far away I think, "Man, I should have gotten that thing!"

My business partner, Albert, likes to point out, as he calls it, "the power of the cane." In a crowded airport or packed flight he'll say, "Use the power of the cane and get us boarding early." People tend to come running to "help" when they see my cane! In a busy hotel he says my cane is like Moses and the parting of the Red Sea: People jump and scramble out of my way as I calmly walk through! I just have to laugh at times like those!

There are times in the professional environment when things are not made accessible for me so I like to have some fun with my sighted colleagues at meetings now and again. I will have a handout and give out just the Braille copies. Then I will say, "Oh you know what, I meant to print some copies for you guys but I ran out of time. You can just listen as we go through the agenda."

Seriously, being blind forced me to realize that while I am artistic by nature, a "creative," I am not innately organized. I had to learn to get organized and focus. I need to know where stuff is. I can't just throw things down; everything has to have a place. Before I was married I lived alone. I would miss trains to work because I couldn't find my cane. Can you imagine having to tell your boss you are late because you couldn't find your cane? No, I had to get organized, and that has served me very well. I am definitely far from the most organized person. It is still a challenge for me, but being organized has helped me be successful. It's organize or perish.

People who can see don't know how much they tell you by how they say things. They might be very good at guarding how they look, what their expression on their face is, but sometimes if you hear them talk you can tell that maybe they are not saying the whole truth or maybe they let more of their feelings show through their voice than other people will pick up. I can pick up on that.

All in all, it is important to know that the world is bigger than any one of us. We have to find where we fit in and where we can help other people. None of us, sighted or blind, can "do anything we want to do." The secret lies in finding what we can do well and what we want to do well and then learning how to do it as well as we can.

Breaking Blind

The Story of Maureen Nietfeld
Teacher of Daily Living Skills for the Blind
and YouTube Show Host

When I first chatted with Maureen Nietfeld I thought to myself: She is in the perfect career. I had only known her for a little while in a phone conversation, but I could tell that if I had a crisis or needed someone to teach me a new way of doing something, Maureen was the person. She has a cool, unpretentious way about her, and I could tell she enjoys guiding people, being by their side, and showing them the ropes of the challenges she helps them overcome. I have to say it literally makes me laugh out loud to think that Maureen is teaching people how to accept blindness by learning living skills. Just wait until you read her account of how she handled blindness and of learning the skills of blindness in her teens—her oh so typical teen years!

I was introduced to Maureen through Cheryl Locker, one of the Teachers of the Visually Impaired who worked with my boys in our town of Bucks County, Pennsylvania. Cheryl also worked with Maureen back when she was in high school in a neighboring district a few years before my boys came along. When I mentioned I was creating this book, Cheryl's face lit up as she excitedly told me, "You have to meet Maureen!" I am so grateful she connected us because Maureen's journey is one that I love sharing.

Maureen is totally blind. Knowing that, let's just take in her current careers: Teacher of Daily Living Skills for the Blind; sounds appropriate and perhaps cliché, yes? Somewhat of a blind leading the blind perhaps? It's perfectly reasonable and not surprising that Maureen is successful with it. Her additional career is my personal favorite: YouTube star! At first I was happy to interview Maureen because she knew a lot of the teachers I know. When I found out she has a successful YouTube channel, I was surprised and intrigued. My younger son, Mitchell, was just becoming obsessed with making YouTube shows, and I thought it was a lost cause! I mean, really, a blind person creating shows on an all visual platform? Tune in to Maureen on YouTube and you will see the answer is WHY NOT?!

In listening to Maureen talk about her work, what I love most is her passion for fitness in the blind community. Maureen uses her YouTube channel and her position at the Colorado Center for the Blind to educate and motivate blind people to get active. Not surprisingly, Maureen and I ended up talking about the National Center for Disabled Sports. Maureen works with the folks at this incredible center, and my boys skied with them a few years ago. We both excitedly agreed it is a magnificent center with wonderful programs, but Maureen cautioned me that while she loves when blind people have outings to places like that, she really wants to see them including sports and fitness into their everyday lives. I couldn't agree more.

Enjoy reading about Maureen's journey; she offers so many wonderful lessons about acceptance with fun stories along the way!

How Maureen Sees It

I work at the Colorado Center for the Blind where I teach people the skills they need to be successful in life as a blind person. I teach home management (or daily living skills). Cooking, cleaning, grocery shopping, budgeting, putting on makeup, ironing clothes—I teach the things students need to learn to make them independent in their home life. Since I am blind myself, I can actually say I know what my students are going through.

I grew up in suburban Philadelphia in Bucks County, and I now live in suburban Colorado. I miss the town I grew up in but, in Colorado, I can get around my area so much easier than back home. I can easily access two bus lines and the light rail, which connect the suburb I live in to the Denver metro area. The access is fantastic, and the weather and the people here are wonderful.

I was born sighted. When I was four years old, my mom took me to the eye doctor because she thought maybe I had a lazy eye or something. My one eye wouldn't focus the right way, and it seemed like I bumped into things on my right side more often, and I wasn't able to grab something if it was coming to my right side. So she took me to the eye doctor. It turned out my mom was right: Something was definitely wrong. I had tumors in my right eye.

I then went to see some of the best doctors in the country at Wills Eye Hospital in Philadelphia. There was a suspicion of my diagnosis, and then lots of MRIs to try to confirm it. My diagnosis was not confirmed until I got my first brain tumor at age ten. I was diagnosed with Von Hipple Lindow (VHL) Syndrome. According to Cancer.net, "VHL is a hereditary condition associated with hemangioblastomas, which are blood vessel tumors of the brain, spinal cord, and eye. The eye tumors are also called retinal angiomas. People with VHL also have an increased risk of developing clear cell renal cell carcinoma, which is a specific type of kidney cancer, and pheochromocytoma, which is a tumor of the adrenal gland."

The doctors treated the tumors in my eyes with laser surgeries and cryo treatments. (According to Wikipedia, cryotherapy is the local or general use of low temperatures in medical therapy. Cryotherapy is used to treat a variety of benign and malignant tissue damage.) The surgeries and cryotherapy caused glaucoma and retinal detachments. When nothing else could be done, I had both of my eyes removed.

I was seventeen years old and completely blind. I hated it. I did not want to learn Braille. I did not want a white cane. I didn't want to learn anything that in any way, shape, or form identified me as a blind person. I was ashamed. Now I look back and see that I felt ashamed of something I had no control over, which isn't right, but I was seventeen years old and quite a typical teenager, with thoughts that weren't always rational.

I was so against learning blindness skills that I don't know how Cheryl, my Teacher of the Visually Impaired, survived my bad attitude! My mobility instructor, oh my goodness, poor Jody Vargas, how I drove her crazy! The mobility instructor's job is to teach a blind person how to navigate their surroundings safely and independently. To become skilled at traveling independently you begin by practicing the routes you use most at home, work, or school. Well, I wanted no part of practicing "being blind," and I especially did not want to practice in any place where anyone I knew could possibly see me! I would argue with Jody over where to go for mobility lessons, and I wouldn't use my white cane, ever.

Mobility lessons teach independent travel. The "urban travel" lesson is designed to teach a blind person how to safely travel throughout a city, independently. The key here is *independent*. The mobility instructor gives the blind student a destination, and together they plan a route to get there. The student finds his or her way using the white cane, sound clues, and other techniques to safely make her way. All the while the mobility instructor stays a few yards behind the student, allowing them independence but being available to step in to assist if needed. I remember one time Jody and I went into downtown Philadelphia for our urban travel lesson. On that lesson I was supposed to make my way from the train stop at Market East (Jefferson Station) to a specific address: 919 Walnut Street (at the time it was the Library for the Blind). I was not happy about the lesson. I hated being blind. I hated that I had to do it alone. As I was standing outside the train stop, refusing to try to accomplish this on my own, a woman stopped me and asked if I needed help. I was supposed to make the trek independently. I was supposed to follow a planned route with no assistance. So I said to the kind woman, "Yes! I do need help! Can you walk me to 919 Walnut Street?"

Let's just say Jody was not happy at all. I ditched the whole goal of the lesson (independence) but Jody was more upset, rightfully so, that doing something like that, relying completely on a stranger to guide me, was really dangerous. Asking for help isn't always dangerous, of course, but you have to be careful and learn to navigate as independently as possible so as not to rely on the kindness of strangers.

I would eventually learn the skills of blindness and function well enough to work, cook, clean, and have a social life. People around me thought I was "amazing" as I moved on with my life as a blind person, but the truth is, I wasn't amazing at all. I never went anywhere by myself. I got dropped off and picked up at work (I was a massage therapist). I was not doing anything extra. I wasn't doing anything that I really wanted to do or had the great potential to do. The fact that my doing the minimum of what adults should be doing was considered amazing was shocking proof to me that there are such low expectations of blind people. I had to set high expectations for myself and the life I wanted to have, and I had to immerse myself in a program where I could get the skills I needed and change my mindset to be fully independent and to thrive. I went to the Colorado Center for the Blind and got the training I needed to live the life I wanted. I liked it so much I stayed here!

Now I do anything and everything I want to do. My husband (who is also blind) and I work and travel. We have an extraordinary life because we don't do anything extraordinary at all; we just do the things we want to do! My only wish is that I would have gotten the intense training earlier, but I guess life is full of "would'ves and should'ves." I believe everything happens for a reason, and my life is playing out just as it was supposed to.

What I have learned living and working as a blind person is the importance of Braille. In my experience, adults that are Braille literate are much more competitive in

> *We have an extraordinary life because we don't do anything extraordinary at all; we just do the things we want to do!*

the workplace. In adulthood, Braille is more than just a way to read and write; it also gives you the ability to label your things and write notes to yourself, little things that make things more accessible. I notice such a disadvantage for people that lost their sight later in life and have to learn Braille. I will admit it is difficult to learn later in life but it is doable, and it so effective to learn it! Naturally, then, children that are blind have such an advantage in learning Braille early on. The earlier they learn, the more fluent they tend to be.

Another important skill, a life-changing skill for me, is independent travel. Learning to travel independently changes your life as a blind person. To be able to get around and not have to depend on anyone is huge. I think the biggest upset I had about losing my sight was that I went from being independent and doing what I wanted to then feeling so dependent on others and always going places with someone else. I always needed a sighted guide. I always needed a person there for security. When I went to the Colorado Center for the Blind and I learned how to use a cane and how to get around on my own and how to take a bus and a train and navigate the world again, it transformed me. Well, actually, it made me who I was again. So it transformed my life as I then felt like myself again.

Believe me, I know it's scary. Learning to navigate the world without sight is probably one of the scariest things that you will have to do. I can't speak for someone who has always been blind because they have always been navigating without sight, but for those that lose their sight, it is terrifying for a lot of people. Once you get the training you need in the tools that will help you, however, then you can get on with the life you want to live. Will it be frustrating? Of course! Everybody, whether blind or sighted, gets frustrated with things in life. Blindness is a part of who we are and sometimes blindness causes frustration—the key is to not let that stop you.

> *The cane...is like there is a big flag saying "Here I am. I am blind. I have a cane. I am different." Staying with those feelings gets in the way of learning proper cane travel and moving on to independence.*

I recently led a philosophy class about the white cane and the challenge so many visually impaired people have with using it. For those who struggle with accepting their blindness, many tend to fight using the cane. It has so much to do with the fact that the cane is the defining symbol that you are blind. You are definitely blind, no pretending, no doubt about it. For lots of us, there is the added emotions regarding the feeling that the cane signals you are different. It's like there is a big flag saying "Here I am. I am blind. I have a cane. I am different." I think all of that is okay, but staying with those feelings gets in the way of learning proper cane travel and moving on to independence. So although it's hard, it's frustrating, and it's emotional, move on from those feelings. Don't let them stop you in your tracks. Acknowledge it and move on in spite of it.

I actually don't think this is just a "blind thing." I mean, people, blind or sighted, **people are people;** they go through things. We need to go through what we go through, but we can't stay stuck in it.

I am passionate about making sure that blind people are active. We see such a high obesity rate among people with disabilities as a whole. Unfortunately, the disability population tends to live sedentary lifestyles, which many times leads to obesity, and then poor health as a result. I never really knew this until I started working with this population. I grew up sighted and played all kinds of sports so I was always active, just like the rest of my peers. Now I teach fitness classes to blind adults, and I meet people in their thirties that have no idea how to do a jumping jack or even a bicep curl! So many blind children are excluded from gym class and excluded from regular sports that they have no idea about these kinds of things.

I see wonderful programs offered for blind people to try sports like rock climbing and tandem cycling, and I appreciate that people spend a day taking part in that. They are fantastic ways to experience new things and gain confidence, but my passion lies in teaching blind people to incorporate regular physical activities into their lives. We offer yoga, cardio dance, and martial arts at the Center, and I want to expand our programs. I am working with a program called We Sit Wellness. They work to make exercise affordable and achievable and accessible.

I have a YouTube channel dedicated to empowering and educating blind people. I know it sounds odd that a blind person has a blind audience on a platform as visual as YouTube, but there's pretty much everything on there! I gear a lot of my videos on my channel toward wellness with episodes dedicated to healthy eating, recipes, and workouts. My message is that just because you don't have vision does not mean you cannot have a healthy, *daily* lifestyle. It is an especially important message for children because the alternative to a healthy lifestyle is to grow into adulthood with medical conditions.

The Bright Side

I remember being a kid and either not liking or not wanting to associate with other kids simply because of their "look." I was like all kids in trying to find where I fit, and I really only stayed with the people that were just like me. Now I don't judge people like I used to. When I meet someone, I have to get to know them because I cannot see and make an assumption of where they "fit." I am quite perceptive in "seeing" who people really are and can tune in to their intentions because I am not distracted by or fooled by an outward appearance. Losing my sight has enabled me to see people for who they really are, and that has created many new relationships for me that I otherwise would have missed out on.

It is just so neat for me to get emails and messages from blind people from all over the world! My online work with YouTube and Facebook has reached so many people. It's wonderful to connect with them and have an impact on their lives.

Teach Them Well

The Story of Kathy Nimmer
Teacher of the Year, Indiana 2015

In 2015, Kathy Nimmer was named "Teacher of the Year" in Indiana and also made the "Top 4" in the country. When I talk with Kathy, I find myself wanting to convince her to move to my town and be my children's teacher—all three of them! I know a great teacher when I see one, and I actually planned my whole life to be one of the greatest teachers ever. That plan took a bit of a detour when I found myself having to teach my boys blind skills and teach others how to be inclusive. So when I talk to Kathy and hear her passion and love of the profession, combined with her incredible accolades and accomplishments in the field, it makes me want to convince her to move nearby and impact my kids and their friends on a daily basis!

The funny thing is that I have to remind myself when I chat with Kathy that she is the best of the best. "Teacher of the Year" is such an honor, but Kathy is so humble about it. The only time the "title" comes up in conversation is when Kathy excitedly talks about all the opportunities she has had from being the teacher of the year and acknowledged as top in the country. She gets to travel a lot and impacts tons of other teachers as well as even more children. My personal favorite part: With every encounter, every workshop, every speech, she is showing people just how much blindness is not a big deal.

I admit when I first learned about Kathy I had to know more because, as a former teacher myself, I just couldn't imagine how she could do it and do it so well. I am not talking about maneuvering a classroom, calling on children, no, not those things. I have enough experience with my boys and other blind people to know that there are tons of ways to work around simple stuff like mobility and knowing who is talking. No, I mean things like grading tests, giving feedback on written projects, putting a classroom together. There are so many visual things involved in teaching! My curiosity was in overdrive, but every time I chat with Kathy she effortlessly and so eloquently reminds me of why I loved teaching and why she is so good at it. Systems are important for making a classroom flow, and every teacher develops systems unique to them. The real measure of a successful teacher, though, is her or his ability, talent, and passion to inspire children and guide them to achieve their greatness.

Kathy achieves that on a scale that I could only dream about.

How Kathy Sees It

I was initially diagnosed with Stargardt disease, which is an inherited disorder of the retina, also known as juvenile macular degeneration (per National Eye Institute www.nei.gov). When I went to a conference for that disease in search of information, however, I felt like a misfit. There were too many facets of the disease that just didn't match what I was experiencing. I went in search of a better diagnosis and finally got it. I have a condition called cone-rod dystrophy. (The National Institutes of Health define Cone-rod dystrophy as "a group of related eye disorders that causes vision loss, which becomes more severe over time" [per www.nih.gov].)

I had gradual vision loss until it was pretty much gone by age twenty-three. I now have just a little bit of light perception.

I am a teacher, and for as long as I can remember I had always wanted to teach. When I was first losing my vision as a child, I was forced into working with my teachers more closely because they had to adapt materials for me or read things to me. So I guess because I was so highly engaged with teachers, it just came naturally that teaching was always something I wanted to do. I didn't necessarily have a specific subject area or age group in mind, it was just teaching in general that was always on my radar.

Seventy percent of blind people are unemployed, but as a little girl I never knew that. I had no idea the employment odds were so stacked against me. In my upbringing, it was never a question that I would find a career and work my tail off in that career. I never had a doubt—to the point where I was kind of naïve about how to do it! I knew I wanted to be a teacher but I didn't plan out a bunch of strategies or worry about the ways in how I would make it happen. I knew I could get there, and I got there; but before I got there I had to figure a whole lot out to realize what I needed to do to make it successful. There was never a doubt in my mind, however, that I could accomplish my dream because my parents and teachers never expressed any doubts to me.

In 2015, the teachers in my building chose me as the Teacher of the Year. That led to the district competition. I was in the running with a teacher from each of the other eighteen schools in the district. I won that competition and then went on to compete with winners from the entire state! In the state competition I had to prepare a twenty-one-page portfolio, and as a result I was selected to be in the top ten, which meant I would have to then participate in an interview with the competition committee. I didn't hide my blindness at all up to that point; as a matter of fact, it was pretty clear in my portfolio that I am blind. I don't believe it helped or hurt me in the competition. My blindness is just a part of who I am, like someone's sense of humor or a love of reading. I don't hide my blindness, and I don't trumpet it; it is what it is.

Once the interview came, there was no denying my blindness at all. They saw me in person, and they saw my guide dog. From the interview I was selected to move on to the top three, which meant a classroom observation. The committee got to see me in action moving around my classroom, working with the students, using things like my Braille note notetaker, just doing what I do.

Then I was chosen as the "Teacher of the Year" for my state.

In this role, I actually took a sabbatical from teaching in the classroom to spend a year traveling around the state

---

When logistical challenges are removed, there is more room and opportunity for us to be successful.

---

meeting with teachers and working with the statehouse on education legislation. Essentially, I was a teaching ambassador for the year, and my calendar was full of all things like that. Sabbatical is a misleading term; I was extremely busy and didn't get much rest! It was a totally different thing than the classroom.

My speaking and presenting calendar is actually more full than any other teacher of the year winners that I know. My presentations are not just appealing to adults; the kids can learn so much from me when I show them my guide dog and inform them about blindness firsthand. That's my favorite part!

The sabbatical activities presented only one challenge: travel. The only accommodation I asked for was to fund a driver because obviously, I can't drive. The state never hesitated. They worked with me on how much money the driver should be paid per hour, and it has worked just fine. I have a driver to rely on, and I can do what I need to do. In addition, they funded a companion traveler to assist me on the five national trips I was required to take where all of the state Teacher of the Year winners gathered for trainings and collaborations. For the first couple of national events I definitely needed someone to go with me to assist in navigating the event with so many people I didn't know, but as the year went on I got to know so many of the state teachers that I didn't have to rely on assistance from my travel companion as much. It really worked out well to have support for when I needed it to just get things done more efficiently, but I was able to be quite independent as well.

Being independent is very important to me. I believe independence is a balance between doing things on your own and knowing exactly when asking for help from somebody would make it easier to focus on the bigger thing. I came to understand that when I started using a guide dog. I could use the cane or sighted guide or even trailing the wall to get from one part of my school to the other, but for me those techniques take more focus, more time. When I have the dog, he can get me from place to place, with my guidance and awareness, so I have more time and focus to concentrate on the bigger things like being a good teacher, being available to my students, and being a supportive colleague.

For things like a guide dog and boarding a plane early, those things don't diminish from independence. Those things take care of some logistical issues that would just be complicating the scenery somewhat. When logistical challenges are removed, there is more room and opportunity for us to be successful. So I don't see tools of independence as any kind of contradiction. Those tools don't take away my independence; they clear the horizon so I can focus on the things that really matter.

For those parents whose child is diagnosed as blind, I

want you to know it's okay to be shocked and stagger for a while. It is even okay to grieve the loss of what you had pictured your child's life would have been. I don't mean grieving, like blindness, is a death; however, it is just a different journey that you will be on, a different path you will take. Your child can still absolutely get to the top of the mountain, but blindness is going to change the pathway from what you had imagined for them.

People need to realize that blindness is a sensory disability; it does not affect the brain, the potential to dream, or the will a person has. Blind people just need to be creative and find different pathways to making their dreams come true. Finding that different path takes effort and perseverance. As I mentioned the numbers are against us. Yes, there is that statistic of seventy percent of blind or visually impaired people are unemployed, but there is still the thirty percent that are working. That number can grow from parents who have the belief that their children can achieve and are willing to help them define their dreams and accomplish them.

You know, children are not aware, on a conscious level, that they are facing such stiff odds for success. I sure wasn't! The children are, however, aware of their parents' reaction to the situation so it becomes even more incumbent upon the parents to have that positive outlook, that supportive presence and sense of encouragement and hope and belief, because the children will shape their drive based on what they see their parents and teachers do and say. Little people are always soaking up what we are thinking and saying and believing, and for a parent of a blind child it is even more urgent that the belief is present and that it's authentic. Kids know when adults are faking it and not being realistic. So parents need to educate themselves; they need to think creatively, and they need to support the dreams their children are cultivating in their own minds.

If I can offer a few pieces of advice to those that are blind and to parents raising blind children: First, communication is huge. I'm a teacher, a writer, and I read voraciously so words, whether they are spoken or written, are huge. Like other blind people, I don't have that ability to make eye contact and read body language so I needed to develop my communication and listening skills to be able to pick up on all of the cues that people give. Also I believe for blind professionals, staying avidly aware and alert and pursuing information in our field is very important. We never want to give an excuse for other people to think that we are less than they are or that we are less capable, and so we want to be reading current information. We want to be honing our skills, and honestly, many times we have to be better than the sighted person at what we do in order to get a chance. It shouldn't have to be that way, but we certainly cannot afford to be worse than the average sighted person at the thing we want to do because that just opens the door for us not to be hired or not to be maintained in a position. So we must work hard and stay current with the skillset that is required for our dreams for our careers to be real.

The Bright Side

I certainly think that blind people have an advantage in getting to know people. We are not judging by appearance. We aren't noticing who is wearing expensive clothing and who isn't, who looks like society says you should look and who doesn't. We have to talk to people and have to get to know them on a personal level. I always feel an advantage with my students in particular. I don't make any snap judgments based on what I see. It may take longer to learn a voice than it would to see what someone looks like, but I think it's a more authentic knowing because we have to be so verbal and interactive. It is essential that we dig beneath the surface where people that have vision might get tripped up in what they see. We have the advantage; we get to know people on a deeper level.

Boarding a plane early is a bright side! I always pre-board because it just makes it easier logistically. Whether I have my dog with me or not, it is just easier to get on there and find everything before there is a whole bunch of people swirling around me.

I taught in the classroom for twenty-three years. Moving on from here, after this experience of teaching outside the classroom, my future will hopefully be a blend of both.

Navigating the Race of Life

The Story of Simon Wheatcroft

Storyteller, Technologist,
Adventurer, Inclusivity Consultant, Runner

Simon Wheatcroft wears many hats. He is an adventurer, runner, and speaker—to name a few. My favorite job title of his, though, is "inclusivity consultant." Inclusivity. Inclusion. Include. When I talk with Simon, those are the words that are the through line of every conversation we have. His passion for inclusion of blind people, of all people, in mainstream life is evident in everything he does. The desire for inclusion runs deep in Simon, and he is running races and campaigns to see to it that inclusion of blind people in all aspects of life is achieved, sooner than later.

When I first talked with Simon he was gearing up to spend a couple of months running one hundred and sixty miles in a desert—and he was completely excited about it. I was intrigued to know what the heck would be exciting about running that far, not to mention running in a desert! Simon was working with IBM to develop an accessible app for runners. Okay, pretty cool. But as I listened to Simon's passion for running, I thought, "Oh boy. We couldn't be more different." I mean, we both are runners. Wait. We both run. Simon is a runner. I am not. I run to clear my head and fit into my jeans. I do not jump out of bed excited to get out there and push myself further, faster, like a runner. Now I can run for hours chasing a soccer ball, but running, just running, with no ball at my feet is not my thing. It is, however, Simon's thing. Simon discovered his passion for running in college, and it has taken him on an incredible journey.

We are definitely different in our reasons for running, but when Simon and I started talking about unemployment rates of blind adults, accessibility, and adapting—when we hit those words in our conversation—I thought, "Oh my, we are so alike!" Simon is just as pissed off as I am about the high unemployment rate of blind adults (seventy percent!). It's invigorating to talk with Simon about it because he sees what I see and what so many blind people see: That ridiculously high unemployment rate has little to do with career options, but everything to do with the fact that people think blind people can't do much.

I encourage all of those that think blind people can't do much to get comfy and read through Simon's journey. If you pay close attention, you'll realize that Simon is just getting started.

How Simon Sees It

I have a condition called retinitis pigmentosa. My vision has declined over time. As my vision has changed, so has my journey. I live in Rossington, Doncaster, UK, with my wife, Sian, and our two children. I currently spend the majority of my time speaking with organizations and consulting with companies about how to customize the user experience so everyone can use the same products. Inclusion and accessibility are passions of mine. In my opinion, if products are designed with accessibility and inclusion in mind, you'll end up with a far more intuitive product that works for everyone.

I was thirteen years old when I first started seeing a doctor for my vision. At age seventeen I was registered as legally blind. I could still see a lot during the day, but not at night. By the time I was in my late twenties, I only had light perception. (Light perception describes the ability to perceive the difference between light and dark, or daylight and nighttime [per www.visionaware.org].)

When I was losing my vision I was angry. I felt like blindness was going to restrict my life. I feared it would hold me back from everything I wanted to do, but what I realized was that I was angry and frustrated because I did not yet have the tools I needed. Once I learned the tools of blindness, I was able to do the things I wanted to do. I use the accessibility options on my Mac computer. I love iBooks and find them to have the best accessibility.

One of the best skills I learned when losing my sight was to adapt, and that skill has served me quite well. I attribute my early adaptability to being in mainstream life. I understood from very early on that I exist in a big wide world that is complicated. I learned to adapt on a daily basis, in lots of different circumstances. Unlike children that grow up in schools for the blind, I grew up in public school with a clear understanding that the world was not perfectly adapted for me; I had to adapt to the world. In many schools for the blind the environment is structured and accessible to make learning as easy as possible for the blind students. It's advantageous on several levels to have an education like that, to have accessibility be a non-issue and full immersion of blindness skills. It certainly sets a great foundation for learning, but what happens when those children get out into the real world where everything is not fully accessible for them? I often think that becomes a big barrier in being able to function. The best programs are the ones that leverage great focus on blindness skills and integration of skills to operate outside of controlled environments, and ideally, very skilled blind people are involved in those programs to model and teach their skills.

All of that said, it is important to consider children that may have additional, secondary disabilities, which is the case for many children that are born with blindness. Those children need careful consideration as to whether a mainstream environment works, or if immersion in a school for the blind serves them better. Just like sighted children, blind children are different. We need to find what works best for the individual child.

Another skill I learned growing up in mainstream schools is my keen ability to socialize with sighted people. I find it important for blind children to know and socialize with other blind children, but they also have to learn to socialize with sighted people. I had so much practice in mainstream school with social interactions with sighted people that I confuse people a lot—they are surprised to find out I cannot see! I got really good at picking up on non-visual cues and making sighted people comfortable with my blindness. People usually don't realize I am blind when I talk to them now.

My ability and enjoyment of being social is probably why I like using a guide dog to navigate, as opposed to the white cane. When I have my guide dog, people approach me. When I have the cane, I feel invisible. People are used to striking up conversation about a dog. The white cane tends to be a barrier for socializing simply because people are just not used to it; it's unfamiliar.

A skill I never learned that I'd find incredibly useful right now is Braille. Honestly, I never thought I would need Braille, but now I am trying to improve my computer coding skills. Using a screen reader solely for coding slows me down. If I were able to use Braille it would be quicker. I am not saying it would be better, just faster. I recently read about Jordyn Castor from Apple. She writes code for Apple utilizing Braille. She is incredibly quick and productive with it as a result of her Braille skills. The predicament I am in now is that if I were to start learning Braille, realistically, it would take me a few years to become as proficient as I want and need to be. That amount of time does not seem like much, but in terms of my career path right now it's an eternity. The lesson here: Learn the skills you need early on in your journey! You never know where life is going to take you. Have many options available to you.

My career path has taken some twists and turns and has definitely been a unique journey. I began my career working with companies like Nintendo and Reebok to build their brands around particular products. I moved on to the educational sector where I worked as a network manager on projects in schools that made learning about computers slightly more interesting. Back in the early days of computer education in schools the main curriculum was to

> *I find it important for blind children to know and socialize with other blind children, but they also have to learn to socialize with sighted people.*

teach how to use Microsoft Word. The company I worked with shifted the focus a bit to teach computer skills that students could actually use when they left school to go out in the workplace.

I moved on to go to University (college) to pursue my interest in psychology. I had planned on a track of clinical psychology, but as I was choosing classes, or modules, I found one on artificial intelligence. I found another on computational math. Suddenly, I found myself exploring many new avenues I had not originally planned on. As I finished my time at University, I did my dissertation on computational neuro science and finished with a degree in psychology. I ended up doing something very different than what I intended, but I adore technology and was happy to be able to stay in the realm of what I love.

During my time at University, I had some spare time between classes and social events. I started running in that spare time. I found that I loved running and continue with it to this day. Eventually, I started using technology for running.

As I was graduating from University I accidentally launched a speaking career! I did a television commercial for Samsung where I demonstrated how blind people could access a particular model phone. The team that created the commercial used drones to shoot it, and that was one of the first commercials to film in such a way. As you can imagine, the commercial got a lot of attention because of the drones, and it started winning awards. The producers of one of the awards shows where the phone was a recipient invited me to speak at the ceremony. It turns out that the audience was composed of just about every tech firm you can imagine. My speech had great impact. I got requests to speak from people that were in that audience, and so my speaking career was born!

While my career has taken off, that isn't the case for most people living without sight. Blind people possess unique skills and abilities that are often overlooked. People usually don't appreciate how far more beneficial we can be in the workplace than not in the workplace. There is so much work being done to address diversity in the workplace, and blindness needs to be added to the list of groups being served in this movement. Did you know the astounding unemployment rates of the visually impaired? Seventy-five percent of blind and visually impaired people are unemployed. I have not seen one report on diversity in the past two years that even mentions blind people, yet I have seen thousands that mention females, ethnicity, and sexuality. It's time to add blind workers to the list.

I have begun working with the Royal National Institute of Blind People (RNIB) to combat this issue and drive progress. While they are very open to working on it, the difficulty is determining what angle to approach it from. From a tech perspective, there is a heavy focus on compliance. I often feel compliance is not the best way to make anything accessible. As soon as you say compliance, everyone groans. It is not really inspiring to make change if all we do is carry a stick that says you have to. I don't see it as a great motivational tactic. Instead, I talk about framing it to make perfect business sense to make things accessible, rather than compliant. In addition, I promote a shift in perception, both inside and outside the blind community, of what it means to be blind, what we are capable of doing. I am creating a network at the RNIB to promote this.

In addition to a change in perception, I believe we need initiatives in the business community to evaluate why blind people are not getting hired and fix it. Are blind people not even considered for positions? Are they given an opportunity to interview? If they interview and are qualified, are companies not willing to make reasonable adjustments if necessary? It is a concept I am exploring now.

The Bright Side

Blindness has made me interact with people differently because I do not have visual cues. I have found that blindness improves your ability to listen; you actually listen to what people are saying and how they say it. Without such a heavy reliance on visual gestures and distractions, I think blindness makes you slightly more attentive to what people are saying.

Without the distraction of sight, I can pick up people's voice patterns and know who people are by their voice. As a blind person, I rarely make judgments based on the way a person presents visually. I am referring here to implicit bias:

"Also known as implicit social cognition, implicit bias refers to the attitudes or stereotypes that affect our understanding, actions, and decisions in an unconscious manner. These biases, which encompass both favorable and unfavorable assessments, are activated involuntarily and without an individual's awareness or intentional control," according to The Ohio State University, Kirwan Institute for the Study of Race and Ethnicity (per http://kirwaninstitute.osu.edu/research/understanding-implicit-bias/).

A lot of people aren't aware of just how often we rely on implicit biases. Everyone has them. I have them, but they are so rarely triggered because I can't see. I recently wrote a blog piece about a new hiring practice called Blind Hiring. Basically, you eliminate things from the application like gender and age so you can work through the interview process with no bias. I argued that a best practice would be to employ blind people to do the hiring because we are incapable of engaging implicit biases. When someone walks in the room I have no idea what they look like, for example, their ethnicity, unless they disclose it. Essentially, because blind people can't see, we have far lower implicit biases that are predominately triggered by what someone looks like. Blind people have an advantage here.

Blind people offer so many advantages in the workplace. There are many blind adults that are working and succeeding in their careers. I believe it's time to scale up now. I look forward to driving progress in this realm.

Fix It and Forget It

The Story of Larry Woody

Auto Mechanic, Business Owner

Larry Woody is the type of guy that you know in the first few minutes of talking with him is a kind soul. He is humble, he is grateful, and he is so wonderful to chat with. I admit that when I first heard about Larry it threw me for quite a loop, I mean, a blind auto mechanic? Seriously? I had been on a quest for several years to expose my sons to stories of folks with and without sight in all kinds of careers but this? I was intrigued and wanted to know more about him.

A few seconds into chatting with Larry and you feel like he's an old friend you are just catching up with. His personality and humor make you feel so comfortable with him, but I think it's how lovingly he talks about his family that connects people to him so easily. Larry mentioned several times how blessed he and his wife are to have wonderful children and grandchildren, and he feels extremely blessed that he sees his family a lot; they all live in the same town.

So here is a guy that was having success in the career of his dreams, one that you immediately think would, of course, require sight. Then he had this horrible accident and loses his sight, and seemingly his career. Although he was motivated to get back to work after the accident, he found out that his boss doesn't want him. I am pretty sure nobody would fault Larry for growing a little bitter, a little frustrated, to say the least, but not Larry! Nope, he made the choice to carry on with what he wanted to do.

Although I so enjoyed talking with Larry every time we connected, I started to get really worried that he was too happy, too unrelatable to folks that would read his story. The goal of these stories is to inspire folks to chase their dreams no matter the obstacles, but I believe I have a responsibility to present the good, the bad, and the ugly about tough journeys. How would Larry's positive plus attitude fit in here? So I asked Larry if he ever struggled in accepting his blindness. He said in a gentle, calm voice, "I'd be lyin' to ya if I said I didn't have some hard times with this." You'll read the story of one of his first attempts at navigating a neighborhood without sight and without his

> *My motto since my accident has been "Life is a choice."*

mobility instructor. This story is not his favorite moment. It goes a long way, however, in helping us understand that even someone as positive as Larry breaks down in struggle sometimes. Larry always makes the choice to get up and get on with things; we can all learn from this motto.

I am not the first one to make Larry's story available, and I am certainly wayyyyyy down in the alphabet from the A-list folks who have covered him. (Larry was featured on the *Katie Couric Show* and in *Popular Mechanics* magazine, to name just a few.) Honestly, when I reached out to Larry I was worried that he would be tired of sharing his story yet again. He told me how much he loves and appreciates being able to get his story out to people. He told me he likes to share because if it gets one person to get off the couch and go and live their life because of it, it is worth every minute.

That's exactly the point of this book: to share stories of

possibility, resilience, and thriving. I am thrilled Larry sees the extreme value in sharing as well.

How Larry Sees It

I don't consider myself a blind person. I consider myself a guy that just goes through life in the dark, and I carry on just like a sighted person.

I wasn't born blind. My vision was just fine. I was living with my wife; my two children and their families were close by, very close by, as we all lived on the family ranch. I was working as an auto mechanic, something I loved to do. One day in 2002 the owner of the shop I was working at asked me a golden question: Where did I want to be in ten years with my career? My answer was that I either wanted to be in a partnership managing someone's successful shop or own my own. He offered a position as head manager of the shop, and I was thrilled.

Then my life changed quite a bit. I was involved in a car accident that broke my back and all of the bones in my face. I was fortunate that my broken bones healed, but I was left completely blind.

My motto since my accident has been "Life is a choice." When I was lying in my hospital bed, a psychologist asked to talk to me so I said, "Sure, I'm not going anywhere." Our conversation went like this:

"How you doing, Larry?" she asked.

"I am sitting on top of the world," I beamed. (My daughter was there and told me the look on the gal's face was shock.)

"How can you say that knowing you are going to be totally blind the rest of your life?" the doctor wondered.

"Well (I checked my legs, my arms, did a body pat down), we're all here. I have a great family and a wonderful group of friends. So I have a choice: Put myself on top of the world or find my burial plot and put me in it. I am not ready for the second so my choice is to go out and make the best of life each and every day and live it the best I can."

My daughter said the gal shrugged her shoulders when she said, "Okay, well, if there's anything I can do to help ya!" And off she went.

That has been my motto. Make choices every day and do the best you can. At the time of the accident we lived on a family ranch. Since my wife and I were in the middle of a kitchen remodel, when I got released from the hospital I stayed with our son for a little while. I started mobility training while my wife was off for the summer (she worked for the school district). When my wife went back to work in the fall there were days when I was the only one on the ranch for the most part of the day, and I just got comfortable being by myself and carrying on with life.

One of the first things I did was climb up a ladder to fix the top of a trailer. My wife was shocked when she got home from work and found out that I had climbed a ladder. Other family members didn't consider it a great idea, either, but I did it the same as if I was sighted! I set the ladder up, got it in place, leaned it over the trailer, and went to work. I didn't put myself in danger of falling off the trailer in any way. I just learned to do things on my own and carry on as much as I could by myself.

Eventually, I got back to working on cars. With automotive repair, so much of it is done by feel. One of the first things I did was put a water pump in my in-laws' Toyota pickup truck. Then I did the rear brakes on my wife's Dodge Stratus, and then I rebuilt an engine slowly, step by step, feeling every piece. Working on cars is something I have always loved to do so it just came naturally to do it all again.

After I healed, adjusted to life without sight, and found that I could still work on cars, I went back to my job to get back to working. The owner would not hire me back. He told me as a blind person I was a liability to him. Turns out it was a good thing he didn't hire me back because my wife and I bought a shop of our own! Our shop did quite well, and we were in the process of remodeling and adding another 1300 square feet to it when my former boss came to see us. He was just amazed at what we were doing, and he was shocked when he learned that I was putting in the same amount of time at my own place as I had put in for him. He sheepishly said, "It was my loss."

Some people are uncomfortable around blind people or anybody that is a little different. I don't understand that. I like to be around anybody. In the first year that we had our own shop, we had an apprentice that was deaf. I looked at him like he was just a regular person that just can't hear. Call it a disability if you want to, but he is just a normal person. He couldn't hear, and I couldn't see but we were both normal people, and we wanted to be treated that way. We had to figure out how to work together. Communicating with him was no problem because he had an interpreter that would be there with him. The interpreter would sign everything I said; he would sign back to her, and then she would tell me what he was signing. The interpreter was his voice. We had a lot of fun together because he enjoyed cars like I did, and he really wanted to work on them. I would spend about two hours a day teaching him the basics of working on cars. It sure did raise some eyebrows in our town, a blind mechanic teaching a deaf student! It worked just fine, and we had a good time.

My wife and I have four grandkids. Our son has two daughters and our daughter has two sons! Our son is in a wheelchair due to a car accident so his daughters and all of our grandkids are completely used to that, which probably helped them adjust so easily when I went blind. They simply said, "Grandpa, we'll help you." Kids aren't bothered by stuff like blindness. They just help you carry on. One time that really tugs at my heart was when my oldest grandson, my wife, and I went out to dinner. My grandson was about five years old at the time, and he got out of the back of the car and came to my door. He said, "Okay, Grandpa, here I'll help you." We walked along together, and I was holding on to his shoulder; he was so small at just five years old. When we approached a curb he told me "step," and I felt that he had stepped up so I knew to step up. When we got to the door, he said, "Ok, here's the door." He had picked all that up watching his grandma help me around a few times. It just really touched my heart. That's how it is with my grandkids. It is just the way of life to them. If they want to show me something, they know to bring it over and put it in my hands where I can feel it or they describe it to me.

You know, when a life-changing event like mine happens to someone, I think the best thing to do is to keep a positive attitude. Obviously, any injuries or disabilities are going to get you down if you sit and dwell on them. If I dwell on the fact that I can't see, yes, it gets me down. So I try to just carry on and not dwell on it. There are times

> *I was fortunate. I knew just how capable blind people were before I became blind myself. I knew that I just needed to have the right attitude and learn what I needed to learn and I would be okay.*

when that's hard for me to do, like when I first lost my vision. I worked with a mobility instructor to learn how to get around when I first went blind. He encouraged me to get out and walk the streets of my town outside of our lessons together. One day my wife and I went to a part of town that had sidewalks so I could practice my mobility skills. I was walking down the sidewalk of one particular street using my cane, my wife following a little behind me, and there were tree limbs hanging right at face level to me. Of course, I didn't see them, and my cane didn't find them because the cane was tapping on the ground. The limbs hit me right in the face. I did not have a great reaction to that. I actually took my cane and started banging on that tree! I was so discouraged and so frustrated. I set my cane on the ground and sat down on the curb and told my wife to go get the car; I was done walking for the day. I just sat there on the curb until she got the car and came back and got me. I did have some frustrating times when I first lost my vision; it was tough to adjust to it. I would be lying if I said I was never frustrated, but I learned to make the choice to move on and let the frustration go.

The Bright Side

I experienced the bright side of blindness well before I actually went blind. A few years before my accident, I was off from work and my wife asked me if I wanted to attend her class's field trip with her. I agreed, and we took a group of students from the school she worked at to the University of Oregon. One of the eighth graders in her class was blind, and he was in the group my wife and I chaperoned that day. I was in awe watching him walk around the University of Oregon like I do in my own backyard! He managed to go along, laughing and joking with his classmates. Then we got to an activity at the indoor track, and he took off his backpack, folded up his cane, and took off around the track with the kids! I wanted to know, "How much vision has this kid got?!" I was told he was totally blind. I couldn't believe it.

A year later I was working at the shop (before the accident) and one of the first customers I got to know was a retired gentleman. We were chit-chatting at the counter one day, and I asked him what he did before he retired. He told me he worked with kids. I asked if he was a teacher. "Kind of" was his response. He explained that he was an orientation, mobility, and day-to-day living instructor for blind people. He told me all about how he trained for the job back in Michigan where he grew up and then he went to the Oregon Commission for the Blind. A year later, after my accident, he would come out of retirement to be my orientation and mobility instructor.

I was fortunate. I knew just how capable blind people were before I became blind myself. I knew that I just needed to have the right attitude and learn what I needed to learn and I would be okay. People are faced with so many choices in a day. All you can do is make the choice you feel is right at that time, go on with it, and make the best of it—right, wrong, or indifferent. The day goes on.

If you've got something you want to do in life, do it.

Empowering People Through Technology

The Story of Tom Wlodkowski
Vice President, Comcast NBC Universal

Tom Wlodkowski's resume is quite impressive. Even more impressive is the fact that he is leading a charge in this country to not only make things accessible to the blind on a large scale, but to actually, as he says, make products that have accessibility so built in that it isn't even a factor to note. In other words, Tom's philosophy is that all products should be designed literally for everyone, and if you design with accessibility in mind, the impact on a "regular" user is huge.

Tom's current project made my boys and I cheer. As Vice President of Accessibility at Comcast, making TV watching accessible to blind people is a priority and quite a success for Tom. The product my family now refuses to live without, XFINITY X1 set-top box, has the capability for the menu and on screen descriptions, channel guide, and other features to be announced to blind viewers. It also navigates the menus by way of voice commands, in addition to the traditional remote control buttons. The bottom line: My boys can now independently navigate the seemingly endless amount of channels and shows at any given time—no more waiting for someone who is sighted to read it all to them. The secondary bonus: All of us love being able to just tell the remote what channel or show we want to watch! X1 and its accessibility features are a very big deal in our house!

I had the opportunity to meet and chat with Tom when we were both speakers at the American Council of the Blind's annual convention a couple of years ago. Tom is one of those people that has great things to say and gets right to the point. Everything he says has such great value.

I love talking with adults like Tom that have been blind since birth because listening to their stories about growing up offers me so much advice for parenting my blind guys! Whatever the current situation is with my blind sons or what we are about to face with school, or other upcoming challenges, I love to find out how others before me made parenting choices. Tom's advice about how his parents raised him was simple: They let him be a kid. Did they worry or have fears? Absolutely. You'll read about a bit of that, but all in all, they put their fears aside and turned him loose to get out there with his three older brothers. I have to admit I cringed at the story he tells about steering a tandem bike (two-seater) from the **front** seat while his dad coached from the back! When I told that story to my older son, Michael, he cheered, literally cheered, because he wants me to let him do the same thing with his buddies. (Um, nope.)

Hence, the importance of a story like Tom's for those of us raising blind children: The more we know from people that walked this path before us, the more we can set expectations, high expectations, for our children to achieve the life of their dreams. The more our children have access to the world through products like the ones Tom is involved in designing, the better.

How Tom Sees It

I was born the youngest of four boys and the only blind

kid in the house. When I was born, my mother told the nurse that my eyes didn't seem right. Although the nurse shrugged it off as nothing to worry about, my mother insisted things were not okay. After all, she defended herself, she had three other children and knew my eyes were not functioning like her other babies. Sure enough, a mother's intuition proved correct.

My blindness came out of the blue into my family so my parents had to find resources to educate themselves on how to raise a blind child. Over time, they joined groups like the Connecticut chapter of the National Association for Parents of Blind Children (NAPVI) and others. Those groups provided good information but most importantly, my parents usually just let me be a kid, and they figured things out along the way.

Now looking back as a parent, what I noticed to be a key factor in my parents letting me just be a kid was that they had to put their fears in the background and let me have as normal a childhood as possible. I remember how I used to ride a bike in my neighborhood. We lived in a typical cul-de-sac community in Southington, a suburban

> *A key factor in my parents letting me just be a kid was that they had to put their fears in the background and let me have as normal a childhood as possible.*

town in Central Connecticut. When I would ride my bike, I would follow another bike rider that was just ahead of me. Mostly I'd follow my friends through the neighborhood, keeping track of where they were headed through casual conversation. When riding with my parents I'd follow their bike, which had a beeping device mounted on the back of the bike seat. I remember one time when I was about six years old and learning to ride with my mom. We were riding around the schoolyard at Flanders School, our neighborhood elementary school. Somehow I fell and twisted my ankle in the wheel of my bike. My mother arrived to help, and once she got me unstuck and calmed me down, I told her that I was done with riding my bike. I never wanted to ride it again, ever. When my mom tells the story of that event she says that at that moment it took every ounce of energy in her to stay strong and not let me give up. It would have been easy for her to say, "OK, Tom. I don't want you to ride either. Let's go home." Instead, she told me there was no other way to get home unless I rode the bike home. "Otherwise," she said, "we would have to stay in the schoolyard all night." Sure enough, I got back on the bike and rode it home, and continued to ride with my brothers and friends for years. At that moment my mother put all her fear in the background so I could thrive.

I remember riding our tandem bike with my dad on vacations in Rhode Island when I was a junior in high school. When tandem biking with a blind cyclist, the blind person is in the back and the sighted person, the "captain," rides in the front and steers, but not us! My dad would let me sit in the front and steer while he was behind me calling out directional information saying things like "slight right," "slight left," "turn right." We would ride down some busy roads. As I think back on it, if people knew what was actually happening (the blind kid steering the bike), they would likely call some children's services agency to step in! Now that I am a parent I asked my Dad, "How could you do that? You must have had nerves of steel. I am not sure I could do that with my son." His response was: "Back then I didn't think about it!"

My parents didn't know everything there was to know about raising a blind child, but they did know how to let a kid be a kid. Years ago I was at a conference and a parent of a blind child told me he wouldn't even let his child pour milk. I asked him why. His answer, "He might spill it." Seriously? I was shocked. My advice to him was to let the child pour the milk! Other kids that are sighted have spilled milk. Quite frankly, even if he spills it a few times, eventually, he will learn the technique of when to stop pouring!

After graduating from Boston College with a BA in Communications, I started my career in the operations department at the Connecticut Radio Information System (CRIS), a radio reading service for the blind. I then took a job as a newsroom producer for a news talk station in Connecticut. My plan was to make a career in radio, but while looking for a job that would get me back to Boston, I fell into accessibility. I was inquiring about a job at WGBH, a public radio station in Boston. In addition to a radio station, WGBH is Boston's public television station and producer of many renowned children's and primetime PBS programs (*Arthur*, *NOVA*, and *Masterpiece Theater*). One of the folks that I was networking with asked me if I ever looked into what the station was doing in terms of accessibility. WGBH pioneered closed captions and Descriptive Video Service (DVS), a service that adds narrated descriptions of a program or movie's key visual elements into the natural pauses of the program dialog. Description is broadcast on the Secondary Audio Program Channel (SAP) for television. That station pioneered descriptive video service for television, and they were doing it on movies at the time. I went to meet the Director of the descriptive video services, who happened to be a Boston College alum. What was supposed to be a twenty-minute meet and greet turned into a meeting that lasted over an hour. Soon after my meeting, DVS was awarded a grant for an outreach coordinator. I was able to get into the station in that role, which was a great way to get into a respected media outlet with a unique twist, working on accessibility.

While accessibility was not my original plan, twenty-five years later I am now at Comcast, the largest media and technology company in the world. I just came at it from a different angle. You never know where the journey is going to take you, and this is such a cool gig: empowering people through technology. I get to work on great projects like the Olympics and other stuff and try to make them accessible to audiences that may not have had that access before. I take it as a great opportunity to play with a lot of technology, meet a lot of different people, and empower people, too.

Growing up blind and now as a blind adult, I can say that there are a few things, skills, and perspectives that have helped me succeed. For starters, independence is key, but independence isn't just doing things on your own; it is also knowing when to take assistance and when you have to stand firm and not take the assistance. True independence involves understanding what your capabilities are and how to maneuver in an environment. Sometimes the individual who is blind has to realize that if other people are with you, sometimes assistive measures are just easier for everyone. For example, my wife, our son. and I were at Universal theme park. The staff at the first attraction saw my white cane and sent us to the accessible entrance. At first I was frustrated, thinking it was the wheelchair entrance and that doesn't apply to me. It turns out it was a better solution for us to enter the ride because the vehicle we had to get on was not only an odd configuration to navigate, we had to enter it by way of a moving sidewalk. I am perfectly capable to do that but it was much less stressful for my wife to maneuver with our son and me. The alternate entrance eliminated the stress for us and made the ride much more enjoyable for my family.

Independence is important to me, especially independent travel; you have to be able to get from one place to another. I fly frequently so this is especially important to me. When arriving at a destination by plane, the airlines tend to believe it is most beneficial to send a person to meet me at the plane and take me through the airport to baggage claim and then the exit. On the contrary, I find it easier to just independently follow the crowd! I prefer to get off the plane with everyone and walk with the crowd to baggage claim, asking for assistance along the way. By walking with the crowd, I inevitably strike up a conversation with someone or multiple people, depending on how long the trek is. Some people are kind and ask me where I am going and they'll say, "I'm heading that way. I'll go with you." Other times I just ask to be pointed in the right direction.

Unfortunately, I have to practice patience with airlines regularly regarding my independence. Airline staff occasionally offer me a wheelchair because that is likely how they are trained: assistance = wheelchair. Since I am fully capable of walking, I politely say, "No thank you." Some staff are cool with that; others are confused. Once I had a skycap follow me around with a wheelchair even though I said I did not need it. He followed me to the restroom, and I had to stop him and say, "Dude, we are getting into some weird territory here. Stop following me."

The key takeaway here is for people to be respectful of a blind person's independence. I know people want to be helpful, which is great to see in today's world. Now, obviously, if I am going to cross a street and don't hear a car coming, I am hoping someone would pull me back just like anyone would do for anyone else. If, however, someone asks if I need assistance and I decline, people need to respect that.

Technology is a big part of my independence and simply getting stuff done. Blind people need to get to know the technology resources and use them to their fullest extent. There are so many new developments happening in this arena. Things like wayfinding (GPS) technologies— glasses with a camera and beacons working with smartphones and other devices that clue us into our physical surroundings, will become more commonplace, and they are great tools. As long as your cane and/or guide dog skills are in place, you can use technology as a nice companion to basic travel skills.

Great technology skills have helped me tremendously in my career. I use screen reader software that reads what is on the computer screen and my smartphone. I use them on the job as well as for many everyday life tasks. Blind people should take advantage of the technologies available and get adept at them to be productive and independent.

Finally, I believe it's important to be resourceful. Assess everything that is at your disposal at any given time and make the appropriate decisions. Think: How am I going to do this task? If the screen reader is not working, how am I going to get the information I need for a project or assignment? Be resourceful also in connecting with blind adults that can help give advice on different things. I don't find myself or any blind people to be amazing. What I do find amazing is when life hits people hard and they pick themselves up and find the courage to pull themselves together.

The Bright Side

Sometimes you just have to seize opportunities that come your way—no matter how those opportunities present themselves. I had an excellent opportunity that turned out to be quite a bright side for my life. Years ago I arrived at a bus station in Boston to travel to my parents' house in Connecticut for Easter weekend. I approached what was the front of a long line to purchase a ticket and asked someone, "Is this the end of the line?" A woman there at the front of the line began telling me where the end of the line was, until she realized the crowd was apparently looking at her disapprovingly, as if to say, "You are going to send this blind guy to the back of the line?" She felt uncomfortable so she quickly said, "Oh, you can just cut in front of me."

That woman's name is Michele—and she is now my wife!

I have had other positive experiences traveling, thanks to my blindness. Michele always says I don't have the real experience in the airport like the rest of the world. People see the white cane and jump in to help me navigate (as I mentioned earlier, that is not always a plus), and I get to bypass a lot of long security lines. Now I am not a fan of taking all assistance offered because so many times the person offering just thinks you cannot possibly accomplish anything on your own, but there are times it just makes things quicker and easier for everyone if you accept a little help. I mean, hey, sometimes it is wonderful to be able to catch a flight without having to wake up before dawn and spend hours in the security line!

All in all, I think blind people have to consider when to educate people in an unobtrusive way. Educating our community can be indirect: People seeing blind people traveling on a business trip sends a great message of independence and capability. Blind people travel every day, but many people have never met a blind person so seeing them navigate travel is a great learning opportunity. You just never know when these opportunities are going to come up, and although I don't always like getting extra or "special" treatment from people, I do maintain a balance between educating someone and just getting on with where I am going.

Resources

Tools to Succeed Without Sight

This is a "starter list" of resources—it is by no means an exhaustive list! Many thanks to our Facebook friends that helped me create this list. When you find additional resources, please share in our Thriving Blind Facebook community. You can also share resources on Twitter, LinkedIn, and Instagram—be sure to use the hashtag #ThrivingBlind and tag me @KristinSmedley.

Thriving Blind Community on Facebook

- www.facebook.com/ThrivingBlind

Hosted by Author Kristin Smedley. Stories, videos, interviews, and more highlighting the contributors to *Thriving Blind* as well as additional adults and children that are succeeding without sight.

National Blindness Advocacy Organizations

- American Foundation for the Blind (AFB)

www.afb.org

The mission of the American Foundation for the Blind is to create a world of no limits for people who are blind or visually impaired. We mobilize leaders, advance understanding, and champion impactful policies and practices using research and data.

- National Federation of the Blind (NFB)

www.nfb.org

The National Federation of the Blind knows that blindness is not the characteristic that defines you or your future. Every day we raise the expectations of blind people because low expectations create obstacles between blind people and our dreams. You can live the

life you want; blindness is not what holds you back.
- American Council of the Blind (ACB)
www.acb.org
The American Council of the Blind strives to increase the independence, security, equality of opportunity, and quality of life for all blind and visually impaired people.

Connections to Others

- Family Connect
www.familyconnect.org
Family Connect is a website created by the American Foundation for the Blind (AFB) and the National Association for Parents of Children with Visual Impairments (NAPVI) to give parents of visually impaired children a place to support each other, share stories and concerns, and find resources on raising their children from birth to adulthood.

- BlindNewWorld
www.blindnewworld.org
BlindNewWorld is the first-ever blind awareness social change campaign, sponsored by Perkins School for the Blind, to demystify blindness and break down the barriers to inclusion—discomfort, pity, fear, and stigma. Through provocative PSA mini-films, new statistics on public attitudes, compelling stories, and social dialogue, BlindNewWorld seeks to disrupt stereotypes and inspire the sighted population to open its eyes to the full social, professional, and academic capabilities of the blind population.

Technology

- Accessible TV: Comcast Xfinity X1 Talking Guide
www.xfinity.com
The talking guide for Xfinity X1 is a Voice Guidance feature that allows customers with visual disabilities the freedom to independently explore thousands of TV

shows and movies. It "speaks" what's on the screen and includes details such as program descriptions to help you decide what to watch.

• HumanWare
www.humanware.com
HumanWare is the global leader in assistive technology for people who are blind or have low vision. HumanWare offers a wide range of innovative products, including the BrailleNote Touch, the first Google certified Braille tablet: the iOS compatible Brailliant Braille displays; Victor Reader®, the world's leading family of digital audiobook players; the unique Prodigi® family of desktop and portable vision and reading systems; and the ultra-portable explore line of electronic handheld magnifier.

• Apple
www.apple.com/accessibility
Apple devices let you write a text or email without seeing the screen. You can take a perfect group selfie just by hearing how many faces are in the frame. Using these features may feel like magic, but it's very much by design. VoiceOver describes exactly what's happening on your iPhone, Mac, Apple Watch, or Apple TV so you can navigate your device just by listening. Apple's built-in apps support VoiceOver, which will talk you through tasks you do with them.

• Computer Screen Reader (Windows): JAWS
www.freedomscientific.com
JAWS, Job Access With Speech, is the world's most popular screen reader, developed for computer users whose vision loss prevents them from seeing screen content or navigating with a mouse. JAWS provides speech and Braille output for the most popular computer applications on your PC.

Rehabilitation

- Associated Services of the Blind
www.asb.org
Associated Services for the Blind and Visually Impaired (ASB) is a private non-profit organization created to promote self-esteem, independence, and self-determination in people who are blind or visually impaired. ASB accomplishes this by providing support through education, training, and resources, as well as through community action and public education, serving as a voice and advocate for the rights of all people who are blind or visually impaired.

- Colorado Center for the Blind
www.cocenter.org
The Colorado Center for the Blind is a world-renowned training center located at the foot of the Rocky Mountains in Littleton, Colorado, about thirteen miles south of Denver. Since its establishment in 1988, the Colorado Center has provided innovative teaching techniques and philosophy that continues to have far-reaching effects on the lives of blind people, taking them to new heights of independence.

Education

- *Making It Work: Educating the Blind/Visually Impaired Student in the Regular School* (book)
by Carol Castellano available at www.amazon.com.

- Perkins School for the Blind
www.perkins.org
The Perkins mission is to prepare children and young adults who are blind with the education, confidence, and skills they need to realize their potential.

- Texas School for the Blind and Visually Impaired
www.tsbvi.edu

Texas School for the Blind and Visually Impaired (TSBVI) serves as a special public school in which students, ages six through twenty-one, who are blind, deaf-blind, or visually impaired, including those with additional disabilities, are eligible for consideration for services on the TSBVI campus. It is also a statewide resource to parents of these children and the professionals who serve them, from birth through transition from school.

• The Braille Institute
www.brailleinstitute.org
Braille Institute is a non-profit organization offering a broad range of free programs, classes, and services serving thousands of students of all ages to empower themselves to live more enriching lives with blindness and vision loss.

Raising Blind Children

• www.wonderbaby.org
This website is dedicated to helping parents of young children with visual impairments as well as children with multiple disabilities. Here you'll find a database of articles written by parents who want to share with others what they've learned about playing with and teaching a blind child, as well as links to meaningful resources and ways to connect with other families.

• National Association of Parents of Children with Visually Impaired (NAPVI)
www.napvi.org; also www.lighthouseguild.org
NAPVI is a national membership organization that enables parents to find information and resources for their children who are blind or visually impaired, including those with additional disabilities. NAPVI provides leadership, support, and training to assist parents in helping their children reach their full potential.

Facebook Support Communities
- Thriving Blind
- National Association of Parents of Children with Visual Impairment (NAPVI)
- Parents of Blind Children
- For Little Eyes

Medical information (including how eye diseases progress, summaries of conditions, find a doctor)
- National Eye Institute
www.nei.nih.gov
- Curing Retinal Blindness Foundation
www.crb1.org
- Retina International
www.retina-international.org/

Sports for Blind Athletes
- United States Association of Blind Athletes (USABA)
www.usaba.org
The United States Association of Blind Athletes empowers Americans who are blind and visually impaired to experience life-changing opportunities in sports, recreation, and physical activities, thereby educating and inspiring the nation.

- Blind Sports Organization (BSO) Philadelphia
www.blindsports.org
Blind Sports Organization (BSO) provides, promotes, and advocates for sports, recreation, and fitness opportunities for the blind and visually impaired. BSO is a 501(c)(3), non-profit, community-service organization. It has been in existence since 1974 and was formerly known as Pennsylvania Association for Blind Athletes (PABA).

- Camp Abilities
www.campabilities.org
First and foremost, the mission, or purpose, of Camp Abilities is to empower children and teens with visual impairments to be physically active and productive members of their schools, towns, cities, and communities, as well as to improve the health and well-being of people with sensory impairments.

- National Sports Center for the Disabled
www.nscd.org
The National Sports Center for the Disabled (NSCD) is one of the largest outdoor therapeutic recreation and adaptive sports agencies in the world, based out of Winter Park Resort and Mile High Stadium in Colorado. The NSCD is recognized around the world as a premier therapeutic recreation organization, providing leadership and expertise in adaptive sports.

Acknowledgments
Hugs, High Fives, and Fist Bumps

To Kirk, Lonnie, Diane, Michael, Chris, Kay, Scott, Bill, Maureen, Kathy, Erik, Simon, Tom, and Larry: Not only were you each a pivotal person in my journey of raising Michael and Mitchell to rock their life's purpose, your contributions to this book are giving so many more people the inspiration and tools to rock their own life's purpose. C'mon—everyone in for a big group hug.

To the family that welcomed my family with open arms and inspired us to **reach** for greatness, Ed and Erik Weihenmayer: Ed, you so graciously took my phone call so many years ago and have been a role model for me to thrive as a parent ever since. Erik, I need words bigger than the mountains you climb to express my gratitude for sharing your greatness with my family and with the readers of this book.

To my editor and one of my inspirations to become a teacher, Mary Wieczezynski (aka Mrs. Wiz): I find it no coincidence that the person who inspired me to actually enjoy good grammar way back in elementary school is also the person who made sure the grammar is solid in this book. (Let's not mention the fact that my grammar got a tad sloppy in the years between your classroom and this project! #wink) Best of all, though, was all the love you sent with each email. You were my first feedback on a very vulnerable work, and I am so grateful for your kindness and applause.

To my secondary editor and one of the greatest friends a girl could ask for, Sue Schneider (aka Mom): Your effort to make sure all the edits from Mrs. Wiz actually made it to the final copy was astounding. Your effort in keeping me organized is sooooo keeping Staples in business.

To my cover creator, Eric Labacz: It's funny to realize that saying goodbye at eighth grade graduation from St. Ephrem School a zillion years ago was not actually a final goodbye. Thank goodness for Facebook and our reconnection to work on this project! Your talent is incredible, and I am honored that you shared your expertise with me and everyone that this book touches.

To my TEDx coach, Tricia Brouk: The TEDx Talk began my incredible journey of communicating the power of a change in perception to the world and provided a wonderful launch pad for this book. Your work with me during the most difficult time in my life yielded one of the greatest works of my life. You taught me how to talk in a way that inspires people to learn and grow and above all, change. The impact of your talent will resonate for a very long time. I count you in my blessings every time I take a stage.

To my biggest cheerleader of all time, my dad, Rich Schneider: I can't even count how many pounds of meatballs and meat sauce you delivered to my kitchen in the years it took to complete this book. My kids and I are quite blessed to have you as the guy we measure the magnitude of a man against.

To my lifelong friends/teammates Moe, Ellis, Erinhead, and Shannon: Who knew that the soccer fields we met on as kids would be the foundation for which we built lifelong friendships. I would not be the mom or woman I am without your love, support, and fabulous group texts. We may not kick a ball as far as we used to, but we've created some kick-ass lives, and I am grateful and proud to have you on my team forever.

To my Zeta Tau Alpha sisters and dinner dates for life, Staci and Susan: From our very first conversations at West Chester University to ZTA functions and formals to a bottle (or two!) of wine now, you've been my shoulders to cry on, my sounding board for decisions, and most of all my reasons for waterproof mascara as you make me laugh so much. A lifetime's not too long to live as friends. ZLAM.

To my birthday twin Silvia: You are one of the strongest, greatest women I know. I am so grateful that the YMCA brought us together and that Maureen M. Welch Elementary reconnected us. Keep showing the world what resilience and perseverance really look like, my friend.

To the world's greatest texter and best buddy a girl can connect with, Agnes: Navigating the past two years would have looked a whole lot different for me had you not jumped in, raised a glass, and talked me off many a ledge. Your advice, song choices, and nicknames kept me laughing. Newtown is never, ever the same after our visits—it's all in the notes!

To my buddies (aka staff) at Manhattan Bagel in Richboro, PA: Your excitement for my project fueled me even more than all the coffee I drank there while working on it! Your smiles, jokes, and friendship are what make our town a community. My children and I are blessed to live and grow in the community you give so much to.

To my tribe, my chicks, my @4ChicksChatting podcast partners in crime Kathy, MaryFran, and Robyn: You celebrated my ideas for this book, pushed me through the mental blocks, cheered me on through every success and stumble, and nagged the crap out of me to get it done. I believe it's time for another champagne toast...cheers!

To my organizer, brainstormer, cheerleader, and Grammar Police Chief Miriam: I am still in awe that you volunteered to help me get this book into the world. I promise to find a support group for you and Mrs. Wiz to recover from my writing "style." I've stopped starting sentences with "And." Miracles do happen!

To my "Jawn": You keep me laughing through stress and worry. I think you definitely are half man, half amazing.

To my family, my whole, big, crazy family of two parents, four brothers, four sisters, and nine nieces and nephews: In the years it took to create this book you loved and hugged my kids and me through our valleys, and cheered the loudest when we were on our mountaintops. The Sea Isle vacations, birthday parties, hilarious group texts, and especially Christmas Eve celebrations refueled my energy to move forward. You guide my guys when necessary and are living examples of how wonderful full inclusion is. You've taught my children what unconditional love looks and feels like. It is that unconditional love that keeps all of us thriving.

And finally, to the community that has embraced my family, Bucks County, PA: When my boys were diagnosed as blind, I prayed for a miracle. I intended that miracle to be sight. But God had a different plan. He sent me teachers, coaches, principals, Braille and mobility instructors, business owners, neighbors, and friends.

It takes a village to raise a child. It takes patience, love, dedication, and respect to raise a child well. My family has received all of that and more from our town. You allowed me to set the bar high for my children's education and gave us the time and effort to achieve extraordinary things. You made room for my boys on teams and clubs and taught them skills that go well beyond a game or a project. You've added my children to your carpools and party invites. You've prayed with and for us. You've cheered us on and lifted us up. My children now live to do the same. The impact of a thriving circle of love is a beautiful thing to witness.

We. Are. Blessed.

About the Author

Kristin Smedley's mantra is "Life is funny...sort of." Her fun-loving spirit and energetic personality guided her life in the direction of a career in teaching. Kristin fantasized that she would one day be an inspiring third grade teacher, and after earning her degree, she landed her first job in education.

But fate had other plans, and Kristin found herself shockingly dealt a double dose of darkness. Her firstborn son, Michael, was diagnosed as legally blind when he was just four months old, despite the fact that she was advised the chances of having a blind child were one in one million. In fact, only 300 children in the United States shared Michael's genetic mutation.

Once known for her smile, Kristin found herself devastated and angry. Yet fate wasn't finished. Three years later, Kristin received another blow when her second son, Mitchell, was also diagnosed as legally blind at four months of age.

Before the birth of her babies, Kristin had never known a blind person. The boys' retina specialist informed her family that both children would need white canes to navigate the world, and that neither of them would likely ever attend a normal school, pitch a baseball, drive a car, or be able to secure a great job. With no idea how to navigate their needs, Kristin saw little hope for their future.

Nearly suffocating from her own fears, Kristin knew she needed to overcome the anxiety, worry, and obstacles for the sake of her sons, but she had no idea how to proceed. Yet, knowing that Michael and Mitchell needed their mother to fight for them, Kristin began advocating for the tools her blind children needed.

As Kristin found and equipped her boys with the resources to help them thrive, they not only took on the world, but changed Kristin's perception of blindness. With the right foundation and a multitude of resources and tools, her children have become popular, accomplished athletes, high-achieving students, talented musicians, and International Braille competition finalists, as well as typical big brothers to their sighted sister, Karissa, both teasing and supporting her as big brothers do!

In 2011, Kristin launched a mission to fund research and resources for children living with the rare eye disease her sons have. In less than eight years, the Curing Retinal Blindness Foundation has raised over a million dollars and achieved the first legislation in US history to be submitted in Braille—legislation that advocates for better resources for blind and visually impaired Americans.

In 2016, Kristin's blog about changing people's perceptions of blindness went worldwide and was followed by her 2017 TEDx Talk on setting extraordinary expectations. She partnered with Comcast media to spread awareness of the inclusive X1 product. Kristin was one of twelve people in the world invited to testify before the US Food and Drug Administration to advocate for the approval of the first-ever gene therapy to reverse blindness. Kristin is currently the Pennsylvania Ambassador for the National Organization of Rare Disorders (NORD).

Kristin, Michael, Mitchell, and Karissa now mentor families living with blindness, and Kristin's public speaking engagements, book, and social media outreach teach others to move past their fears and obstacles to achieve extraordinary outcomes. You, too, can set extraordinary expectations and achieve your dreams. Please read and share Kristin's story!

Connect with Kristin:
Facebook: www.Facebook.com/ThrivingBlind
Twitter: @KristinSmedley
Instagram: @KristinSmedley
LinkedIn: www.LinkedIn.com/in/KristinSmedley
Website: www.KristinSmedley.com

About the Cover

The cover of *Thriving Blind* was created by artist and designer Eric Labacz. Eric designed it around the painting of the eye that is seen in the center. The painting was created by artist Austin Moran, the son of author Kristin Smedley's lifelong friend and soccer teammate, Dr. Christine (Ellis) Moran.

Austin created the painting for a special event that Kristin hosts annually for the Curing Retinal Blindness Foundation (CRBF). The CRBF was co-founded by Kristin and other parents whose children are blind or visually impaired due to a mutation in the CRB1 gene. The mission of the CRBF is to fund research to better understand and eventually treat CRB1 retinal disease, and to provide resources for those affected by blindness. CRBF is the only patient organization in the world for CRB1 LCA/RP.

Kristin and her CRBF team have raised over 1.2 million dollars. At one of her first CRBF awareness/fundraising events, she invited all attendees to dip their thumb in paint and make a mark in the center of Austin's eye painting. They essentially "put their thumbprint on the mission" to symbolize a long-term commitment to the mission of the CRBF. Since that event in 2011, the CRBF has made a worldwide impact in the rare eye disease field.

To learn more about the Curing Retinal Blindness Foundation, visit www.crb1.org.